politics

Peter Joyce

D1267879

TEACH YOURSELF BOOKS

Dedication

To my wife, Julie, and my daughter, Emmeline.

Long-renowned as the authoritative source for self-guided learning – with more than 30 million copies sold worldwide – the *Teach Yourself* series includes over 200 titles in the fields of languages, crafts, hobbies, sports, and other leisure activities.

A catalogue record for this title is available from the British Library

Library of Congress Catalog Card Number: on file

First published in UK 1996 by Hodder Headline Plc, 338 Euston Road, London NW1 3BH

First published in US 1996 by NTC Publishing Group, 4255 West Touhy Avenue, Lincolnwood (Chicago), Illinois 60646 – 19975 U.S.A.

Copyright © 1996 Peter Joyce

In UK: All rights reserved. No part of this publication may be reproduced or transmitted in any form or by any means, electronic or mechanical, including photocopy, recording, or any information storage and retrieval system, without permission in writing from the publisher or under licence from the Copyright Licensing Agency Limited. Further details of such licences (for reprographic reproduction) may be obtained from the Copyright Licensing Agency Limited, of 90 Tottenham Court Road, London W1P 9HE.

In US: All rights reserved. No part of this book may be reproduced, stored in a retrieval system, or transmitted in any form, or by any means, electronic, mechanical, photocopying, or otherwise, without prior permission of NTC Publishing Group.

Typeset by Transet Limited, Coventry, England.
Printed in Great Britain by Cox & Wyman Ltd, Reading, Berkshire.

Impression number   14 13 12 11 10 9 8 7 6 5 4 3 2 1
Year   2000 1999 1998 1997 1996

CONTENTS

Preface

PREFACE

This book is designed as an introduction to the study of politics. It is aimed at both the general reader with an interest in the subject, and those embarking on an academic investigation.

As an introduction, the material presented in this work is selective. It concentrates on the institutions of government and the political systems operating in First world (or post-industrial) liberal democratic states. It seeks to provide the reader with an understanding of the operations of liberal democratic political systems and the differences which exist between them. The key issues which are discussed are supplemented by a range of examples drawn from a variety of relevant countries. The final chapter raises a number of contemporary concerns affecting the operations of such political systems.

Each chapter contains a summary of the main points which are raised and a number of questions which are related to these. The aim of these questions is to encourage readers to further their studies especially by relating general concerns to specific countries with which they are familiar. This may be done, for example, by reading newspapers and journals in conjunction with this work.

It is hoped that this introduction to the study of politics will encourage readers to pursue their investigations further. A list of more specialised texts is suggested in the conclusion to facilitate this.

Peter Joyce
September 1996

1

KEY ISSUES IN THE STUDY OF POLITICS

Definition

What is politics?

We are all familiar with the term 'politics'. It is encountered in the workplace, perhaps in the form of 'office politics'. We talk of the 'political environment' which fashions the content of public policy. But what exactly do we mean by 'politics', where do we start a study of it and what areas do we need to examine?

Human relationships are crucial. Human beings do not live in isolation. We live in communities. These may be small (such as a family) or large (such as a country). Politics embraces the study of the behaviour of individuals within a group context. The scope of its study is broad and includes issues such as inter-group relationships, the management of groups, the operations of their collective decision-making process, and the implementation and enforcement of decisions. Conflict and its resolution is a particular focus of political analysis. The study of politics thus involves a wide range of complementary subject areas which include political theory, political history, government and public administration, policy analysis and international relations.

Below we discuss a number of key issues which relate to the study of politics. These are usually referred to as 'concepts' and provide us with an underpinning on which a more detailed examination of the political process in liberal democracies can be built. The concepts which are discussed here have particular relevance to the status of the individual in a liberal democratic state.

Political culture

What is political culture and why is it of relevance to the study of politics?

We expect to see a number of common features in a liberal democratic political system. These include institutions such as a chief executive, legislatures and courts, organisations such as political parties and pressure groups, processes such as elections and the possession by individual citizens of a range of personal freedoms. However, their composition, conduct, powers, relationships and operations differ from one country to another. Within a common framework, the workings of the political system in each liberal democracy are subject to wide variation. In France, for example, there is a wide degree of tolerance for conflict as a means of settling political disputes. In Sweden, however, the spirit of compromise tends to guide the actions of key participants to the political process. In Britain there is a tradition of evolutionary rather than revolutionary change.

THE CONDUCT OF POLITICAL ACTIVITY

In assessing the conduct of political affairs, a key distinction needs to be drawn between conventional and extra-parliamentary political activity. This enables citizens to articulate their views on political matters and is an essential feature of liberal democratic political systems – the main characteristics of which are discussed in Chapter 2.

Conventional political activity views a country's legislative assembly as the key arena in which political decisions are made. Elections are viewed as a mechanism through which policies are either initiated or endorsed by the electorate.

Extra-parliamentary action views activity undertaken outside of a country's legislative assembly as a major way of influencing the policy-making process. Methods such as demonstrations, industrial disputes and even riots may be viewed as legitimate mechanisms to achieve political goals.

The level of support for conventional or extra-parliamentary political activity as an agent of change is determined by a country's political culture. Extra-parliamentary activity has traditionally been more acceptable in France, for example, than in Britain.

These variations arise from what we term 'political culture'. This refers to an underlying set of values held by most people living in a particular country concerning the key features governing the way in which the political system should operate. These attitudes influence the conduct of political activity by both politicians and the general public. When we refer to a country's political culture we are emphasising the similarity of views held within any particular country. We are suggesting that within any one country there is a tendency for the majority of persons to think, feel and act in a similar manner concerning the operations of the political system. But these may be quite different from the core values espoused by citizens in another liberal democracy.

ALTERNATIVE VIEWS CONCERNING POLITICAL CULTURE

Liberal theorists suggest that a country's political culture is fashioned by its unique historical development and is transmitted across the generations by a process termed 'political socialisation'. Agencies such as the family, schools, the media and political parties are responsible for instructing citizens in such beliefs and values.

Marxists, however, tend to view political culture as an artificial creation rather than the product of history. They view political culture as an ideological weapon through which society is indoctrinated to accept views which are in the interests of its dominant classes.

The extent of a common political culture can, however, be overstated. Within any country differences are likely to exist concerning fundamental values related to the operations of the political system. The term 'homogeneity' denotes a wide level of similarity in these attitudes but such agreements are not universal. Factors such as de-industrialisation (which has resulted in the emergence of an 'underclass' in many liberal democracies) or immigration (which has led to the development of multi-ethnic societies) have fundamental significance for the existence of universally-agreed sentiments underpinning the political system. Such may give rise to a heterogeneous society (in which dominant attitudes are challenged by subcultural values) or result in a looser attachment to mainstream values possibly resulting in public disorder or revolution.

States and governments

What is the difference between a 'political system', a 'state' and a 'government'?

A political system embraces a wide range of formal and informal processes which exert influence on a state's decision-making processes. These include both the formal institutions of the state but also embrace the influences exerted by individuals and organisations which are not formally incorporated into it. These include public opinion, the media and pressure groups. A political system has no physical dimension or formal existence but embraces a wide range of organisations, bodies and activities whose operations influence decision making.

A state consists of a wide range of permanent official institutions which are involved in formulating and enforcing collective decisions for a society. These usually include the institutions of government, the bureaucracy, courts and police. These decisions are binding on all members of that society and may, if necessary, be enforced by the deployment of sanctions or force in the name of the state. The geographic confines of a state are referred to as a 'nation' or a 'country'.

The term 'government' refers to the institutions which are concerned with making, implementing and enforcing laws. In a narrower sense, however, government is often associated with those who wield executive power within a state. It refers to a specific group of people who give direction to the activities of the state and function as its political arm.

The role of the state

What is the legitimate scope of state activity?

There are widely differing views concerning the desirable scope of state activity. Differences exist both within states over historical periods of time as well as between them concerning the appropriate functions which should be performed. Historically the role of the state was confined to a few key areas which usually included defence and foreign affairs. However, many states with liberal democratic political systems were subject to pressures during and following the Second World War which drastically increased the role of state activity. In Britain, for example, this period witnessed the development of the welfare state, an acceptance that the maintenance of full employment was a proper state responsibility and the placing of several key industries under state control and direction.

INDIVIDUALISM AND COLLECTIVISM

The main difference between these two terms centres on whether the focus of political activity is to serve the interests of the individual or to serve the needs of a group.

Individualists place individual needs at the forefront of their concerns. The aim of politics is viewed as the creation of conditions in which human beings are able to pursue their own interests and thereby achieve self-fulfilment. This is often associated with a reduced role for the state.

Collectivists, however, believe in the sacrifice of self-interest to commonly-agreed goals. Group needs thus supersede individual interests. This often results in the state taking an active role directing the resources at its command to achieve these objectives.

In more recent years, however, political pressures associated with 'New Right' have succeeded in reversing the trend towards increased state activity. In Britain, for example, what was termed 'Thatcherism' sought to 'roll back the frontiers of the state' in both economic and social areas of activity. There are numerous explanations which account for such developments. These include the cost of state activity which resulted in the formulation of policies designed to reduce the overall level of state activity. In the economic sphere, the free market and private enterprise were seen as superior to state control or involvement which was depicted as both wasteful and inefficient.

However, a major impetus for advocating a reduced role for the state was the impact that it was said to have on the individual. It was alleged that those who received state aid (for example, in the form of welfare payments) became dependent on the state and thus relinquished their ability to take decisions affecting the conduct of their everyday lives. The thinking, active citizen had thus been transformed into a passive recipient of handouts while those in employment were adversely affected by the high level of taxation needed to finance the existing activities performed by the state.

Power and authority

Why do we obey our rulers?

A major concern of a government is to secure the obedience of its citizens to its decisions. There are two broad explanations concerning why a government is able to secure popular compliance to its objectives or policies. The first of these is power. Power entails the ability to compel obedience. A body exercising power has the ability to invoke sanctions in order to secure compliance to its decisions. The fear of the sanction thus ensures that the body which may invoke it is able to achieve its goals. A government which possesses power is thus obeyed as its citizens are afraid of the consequences for disobedience. Dictatorships may often govern in such a fashion, executing those who dare disagree with its policies. In liberal democratic political structures coercion is often coupled to resources at the government's disposal enabling it to offer rewards as well as threats to secure obedience.

WHO HOLDS POLITICAL POWER?

There is considerable disagreement concerning the distribution of power within a society.

Pluralists argue that power is widely distributed throughout society and that the role of the state is to adjudicate in the constant competition which exists between competing groups and interests. Decisions thus reflect the process of bargaining between such diverse bodies.

Elitist theories, however, contend that power is concentrated in the hands of a relatively small, organised group of people and that this minority is able to enforce its will on the majority of citizens. Marxists identify the ruling elite as those who possess economic power and are able to use the political system to further their own interests.

The second explanation to account for governments being able to exert control over their citizens is the authority possessed by such institutions. Authority is based upon moral force. An individual or institution which possesses authority secures compliance to its suggestions primarily because there is general agreement that those who put forward such ideas have the right to propose and implement them. Citizens thus obey governments because there is a general consensus that such institutions have the right to take decisions. The content of these may not be generally popular but citizens accept that governments are entitled to initiate them.

Authority may be derived from various sources. In liberal democratic political systems the political office occupied by those who give orders may form the basis of their authority. We accept, for example, that presidents or prime ministers have the right to give orders by virtue of the public positions which they occupy. Such authority may be buttressed by the trust which citizens have in their rulers and the use of symbols (such as the flag) which associate those in positions of authority with interests which transcend secular or party concerns.

In liberal democracies power is usually accompanied by authority. Governments are obeyed in part because there is general consent of their right to govern but also because the courts may be used as a sanction to force compliance to their laws. Power which is divorced from authority is likely to produce an unstable political structure in which violence, disorder and revolution threaten the existence of the government.

The rule of law

What is the 'rule of law' and why is this principle of importance to liberal democracies?

The rule of law is regarded as a fundamental constitutional principle in liberal democracies. It puts forward the primacy of the law as an instrument which both governs the actions of individual citizens in their relationships with each other and also controls the conduct of the state towards them. This principle may be incorporated into a codified constitution (as is the case in America) or it may be grounded in common law (which is the situation in Britain).

THE RULE OF LAW IN AMERICA

The freedom of citizens from arbitrary actions undertaken by government is incorporated into the Constitution. The procedure and practices which must be followed when citizens are accused of criminal actions are laid down in this document, most notably in the fifth and fourteenth amendments. The requirement that no citizen shall be deprived of 'life, liberty or property' without 'due process of law' is imposed as a condition affecting the operations of both federal and state governments. The fifth amendment also provides the citizen with further protection in their dealings with government. No person can be tried twice for the same offence nor be compelled to give self-incriminatory evidence in a criminal trial.

The paramount position accorded to the law as the regulator of actions by citizens and the state has a number of important implications. It suggests citizens can only be punished by the state when they have transgressed the law and that all citizens will be treated in the same way when they commit wrongdoings. Nobody is 'above the law' and the punishments meted out for similar crimes should be the same regardless of where they occurred and who committed them.

Many of the requirements embodied in the principle of the rule of law constitute practices which are widely adhered to in liberal democracies. Citizens are given legal protection against arbitrary actions committed by the state and its officials and the law is applied to all regardless of class, race, gender or creed. However, most liberal democratic states deviate from the strict application of the rule of law. For example, equality before the law does not constitute equality of access to it. Factors which include social background or financial means may play an influential part in determining whether a citizen who transgresses the law is proceeded against by the state and may also have a major bearing on the outcome of any trial.

Questions

1 Identify the key features of the political culture of any country with which you are familiar.
2 'The main aim of political activity is to ensure that individual needs

are fulfilled'. How accurate do you consider this statement to be?

3 Differentiate between the terms 'power' and 'authority'. To what extent are both required by governments in liberal democracies?

4 Define the term 'rule of law'. How important is this principle in the operations of liberal democratic states?

Summary

1 Politics is concerned with the behaviour of individuals in a group context. Its focus includes inter-group relationships, group management, collective decision-making processes and the implementation and enforcement of decisions.

2 Liberal democratic political systems contain numerous common features. The main institutions of government are relatively similar and common features exist such as elections, political parties and pressure groups. However, within a similar framework, the operations of liberal democratic political systems vary from country to country. These differences are explained by a country's political culture which consists of the values underpinning a political system and governing its operations. These underlying values may not be universally subscribed to by all citizens of a particular country: the more they are adhered to, the more homogeneous that country is said to be.

3 Terms such as 'state' and 'government' are often used synonymously but they have different meanings. A political system embraces the wide range of influences which may play a part in a state's decision-making process. These include its formal institutions (such as the machinery of government) and bodies such as pressure groups and the media which are not incorporated into the structure of the state. A government constitutes the executive power which provides the state with its political direction.

4 There is no agreement on the desirable level of state activity. A key distinction concerns whether a state exists to serve the interests of individuals or to meet the needs of groups. State activity is often involved to achieve the latter objective and gave rise to the development of welfare states in many liberal democracies after 1945. The role of the state has, however, been challenged by the 'New Right' in more recent years which sought to 'roll back the frontiers of the state' in both economic and social areas of activity.

5 Governments may rely on power or authority to secure the compliance of citizens to their wishes. Power involves the threat of sanctions to secure such compliance whereas authority entails obedience to a government's initiatives derived from popular acceptance of its right to rule. Liberal democratic governments generally possess both power and authority.

6 The rule of law is a key constitutional principle in liberal democracies. It accords a paramount position to law as the mechanism which governs the conduct of human relations and which regulates the action of the state towards its citizens.

2

LIBERAL DEMOCRATIC POLITICAL STRUCTURES

Definition

What do we understand by the terms 'democracy' and 'liberal democracy'?

A democratic society is one in which political power resides with the people who live there: it is they who are sovereign.

Democratic government was initiated in the Greek city state of Athens in the fifth century BC. The word 'democracy' is derived from two Greek words, *demos* (people) and *kratos* (rule). The term thus literally means 'government by the people'. Initially major decisions were taken by meetings at which all free males attended. It was possible for government to function in this way when the population was small and when the activity of the state was limited. Today, however, ancient city states have been replaced by bigger units of government with a greater range of responsibilities delivered to larger numbers of people. It is necessary, therefore, to find ways whereby the notion of popular sovereignty can be reconciled with an effective decision-making process. We term such a political system 'liberal democracy'.

VARIETIES OF POLITICAL SYSTEMS

Liberal democracies: a key feature of these political systems is that the actions of government reflect the will of the people (or at least the majority of them). To avoid tyranny, the branches of government are separated and its scope is limited. Citizens possess a wide array of civil and political rights.

Socialist democracies: examples of these were found in the former Soviet Union and Eastern European countries. Power was monopolised by the Communist Party and the state's role was to fulfil an ideology and build a society characterised by equality and classlessness. State control of the economy was a prerequisite to achieving this ideal.

Oligarchic regimes: government is in the hands of one person or a small group of people whose rule is maintained by the use of coercion. Civil and political freedoms are typically lacking in such states whose role is to serve the interests of the rulers.

Liberal democracy entails a system in which a small group of people take political decisions on behalf of the general population. Those who exercise this responsibility do so with the consent of the citizens and govern in their name. However, their capacity to take decisions is reliant on popular sanction and may be withdrawn when they lose the support of the population to whom they are accountable for their actions. In such cases the population reclaims its political power and reallocates the responsibility of government to an alternative group of people who subsequently exercise their functions at the behest of the general population.

There are wide variations in the structure of liberal democratic political systems. A major distinction is between those (such as America) which have presidential systems of government and those (such as Britain) which have parliamentary systems. In some the executive branch of government tends to be derived from one political party but in others is drawn from a coalition of parties, perhaps making for a more consensual style of government. These issues are discussed more fully in later chapters of this work.

Political freedom and liberal democracies

What political freedoms are required to underpin the electoral processes of liberal democratic political systems?

Liberal democracies require mechanisms whereby the general public can exercise choice over who will represent them and also to dismiss such persons if they feel that policies lacking popular support are being pursued. This suggests that elections are essential to the operations of liberal democratic political systems. They enable the public to exert influence over the composition of government (especially the legislative and executive branches) and its subsequent actions. They also serve as the means whereby a country's citizens can make a retrospective judgement on the record of those who exercise functions of government.

However, elections are not confined to liberal democracies. Countries with alternative political systems may also utilise them. In October 1995 over 99% of the Iraqi people voted for Saddam Hussein to be that country's president in an election in which he was the only candidate. An essential characteristic, therefore, of elections in liberal democracies is that such contests should provide a genuine opportunity to exert popular choice over the personnel and policies of government. Liberal democracy thus requires a range of political freedoms to serve as the environment within which elections occur. Let us consider some of these essential freedoms.

The timing of elections

Elections facilitate popular control over the activities of government only if they are held regularly and their timing is not totally determined by the incumbent office holders. In some countries, legislators or executives hold office for a fixed period of time at the end of which fresh elections must be held. In America, for example, the president is elected for a four-year term while members of the House of Representatives and the Senate serve for two and six years respectively. Not all countries hold elections at pre-determined intervals. In Britain, for example, the executive has the ability to determine when general elections are held subject to the proviso that fresh elections to the House of Commons must take place at least every five years.

Freedom of political expression

Elections will only provide the public with meaningful political choice if a diverse range of opinions can be articulated. Measures which impose censorship on the media or which place restrictions or bans on political parties, trade unions or other forms of political activity must be pursued extremely cautiously by liberal democratic governments. The freedom of speech, thought and action are essential features of liberal democracies, distinguishing them from more totalitarian systems in which the ability to dissent is circumscribed. An impartial judicial system and freedom from arbitrary arrest are also necessary aspects of such political systems.

Nonetheless, a line needs to be drawn within liberal democracies concerning what members of political parties can say and how they seek to put their views across to the electorate. But what is regarded as acceptable differs from one liberal democratic country to another. Decisions by a government to place restraints on political activities might result in perceived or actual repression which will influence the structure and operations of that party. An organisation which becomes subject to what it regards as restrictive intervention may respond by going 'underground' and adopting a cell structure, the essence of which is covert, secret and conspiratorial organisation and a membership which is highly selective. This may also affect the tactics which the organisation uses. A group which is driven underground may adopt violent means to further its aims. It may become labelled a 'terrorist' group.

TO BAN OR NOT TO BAN?

One reason for banning a political party might be that it does not believe in the basic tenets of liberal democracy: it might achieve power through the ballot box but once installed into power will radically alter a country's political system. On such grounds the 1947 Italian constitution banned the re-formation of the Fascist Party while the French constitution stipulated that political parties must respect the principles of national sovereignty and democracy. A similar provision applies in Germany.

The doctrines espoused by a political party may, further, be viewed as threatening not merely to a country's political system but to the very existence of the state itself. Fear of the Soviet Union and communism (which was believed to be embarked upon a quest for world domination) was prominent in America during the 1950s. The American Communist Party was theoretically banned by the 1954 Communist Control Act, but its enforcement was lax. However perceived sympathy for communism led to discriminatory actions against individuals such as dismissal from employment.

A final reason for banning a political party might be its affect on public order. In Britain, organisations connected with the politics of Northern Ireland using violence for political ends might be proscribed under the Prevention of Terrorism legislation.

The size of the electorate

Popular control over the branches of government necessitates a broad electorate in which the vast majority of the population possess the right to vote. In the nineteenth century the franchise in many countries was based on property ownership: those who owned little or no property were not regarded as citizens and thus were unable to play any part in conventional political activities. The enfranchisement of adults, regardless of wealth, gender or race is necessary for such systems of government to accurately reflect the wishes of their populations.

EQUALITY AND DEMOCRACY

The concept of political equality is an important feature of liberal democratic political systems. Progress towards universal adult suffrage is viewed as a major measurement by which the nature of liberal democracy can be judged. Most liberal democracies, however, deny the vote to some groups of people. In Britain, exclusions include those serving prison sentences. Social or economic equalities are not universally viewed as essential yardsticks of such political systems although the development of the welfare state after 1945 did imply a limited commitment to these alternative goals in some liberal democracies.

The conduct of elections

Elections facilitate public involvement in key political activities only when such are conducted fairly. Factors which include the secret ballot and freedom from intimidation are required to ensure that the outcome of election contests reflects genuine public sentiments. Liberal democracy also requires incumbent office holders to accept the verdict delivered by the electorate and not to oppose it by methods which have sometimes been utilised by non-democratic systems of government. These include setting election results aside by declaring them null and void or supporting a military take-over to preserve the political status quo when an election has demonstrated popular support for fundamental change.

ELIGIBILITY TO BE A CANDIDATE FOR NATIONAL OFFICE

There are a wide variety of regulations in liberal democracies governing eligibility to stand as a candidate for national office. In Britain the qualifications are fairly broad. Any British or Commonwealth citizen (or Irish-born resident) over the age of 18 (with a few exceptions like certain ministers of religion and civil servants) may seek election to Parliament. A candidate merely requires endorsement from 10 registered voters in the constituency he or she wishes to contest and a deposit of £500 (which is returned if the candidate secures over 5 per cent of the votes cast in the election). In other countries the rules are more complex. Candidates may be required to be nominees of political parties which in turn may be subject to controls governing their ability to contest elections. These often require a party to demonstrate a stipulated level of support in order to be entered on the ballot paper. In the 1995 elections to the Russian parliament, for example, each party had to submit 200,000 signatures gathered in at least 15 of the regions in order to enter the contest.

The representative nature of liberal democracies

To what extent do liberal democratic political systems ensure that the opinions of the population are effectively represented?

We have argued that liberal democracy involves a small group of people taking political decisions on behalf of an entire population. But we must consider whether those entrusted with this responsibility are in a position to represent public opinion adequately. There are a number of factors which are relevant to this objective being effectively accomplished.

The development of the party system

We shall discuss the functions performed by political parties more fully in Chapter 4. These may enhance public involvement in policy making, although the extent to which they achieve this is dependent on factors such as the size of the membership of such bodies. Further, the development of party systems may distort the relationship between an elected official and his or her electorate. Voters may support candidates for public office on the basis of their party label rather than their perceived ability to articulate the needs of local electors. While in office party discipline may constrain an official to sacrifice locality to party if these interests do not coincide. The extent to which this happens depends on the strength of party discipline which is stronger in some liberal democracies (such as Britain, Australia and New Zealand) than in others (such as America).

The electoral system

As we shall see in Chapter 3, electoral systems vary in the extent to which the personnel of government accurately reflects the voting preferences of members of the general public. A fundamental division exists between the first-past-the-post electoral system and proportional representation. In Britain, for example, the former has been charged with distorting the wishes of the electorate and producing a legislative body which does not accord with popular opinion as expressed at a general election.

The status of elected officials

Those who are elected to public office may fulfil the role of either a delegate or a representative. A delegate is an elected official who follows the instructions of the electorate as and when these are given. A delegate has little freedom of action and is effectively mandated by voters to act in a particular manner. A representative claims the right to exercise his or her judgement on matters which arise. Once elected to office a representative's actions are determined by that person's conscience and not by instructions delivered by voters. A representative can, however, be held accountable by the public for actions undertaken whilst occupying public office.

THE STATUS OF THE BRITISH MEMBER OF PARLIAMENT

Edmund Burke argued that a Member of Parliament should apply his judgement to serve the interests of the nation as a whole rather than having to obey the wishes of the local electorate.

An MP is subject to no formal restraints on his or her actions once elected. The system of recall which is practised in some American states has never applied in Britain. A Member of Parliament cannot be forced to resign by local electors: their only power is their ultimate ability to select an alternative representative when the next election occurs.

There are informal pressures which may influence the behaviour of an MP, for example the discipline exerted by the party system. But even this may prove an ineffective restraint. In 1995 the Conservative Member for Stratford-upon-Avon decided to join the Labour Party. Neither the Conservative Party nor the local electorate possessed any power to respond to this situation and make him resign. In South Africa, however, members of the National Assembly who cease to be members of the party which nominated them are required to vacate their seats.

The social composition of public office holders

In many liberal democracies the institutions of representative government fail to mirror the make-up of the population by failing to adequately reflect key divisions in society (such as its occupational make-up or its class, ethnic or religious divisions). This is a particular problem for legislative assemblies. Many liberal democracies were slow in according women the right to vote. New Zealand granted this in 1893 and Britain (on a restricted basis) in 1918. However, white, male, middle-class people of above average education continue to dominate the composition of such bodies which are thus socially unrepresentative although possibly reflective of the characteristics required to achieve success in all aspects of social activity. This may mean that the opinions or needs of groups which are inadequately represented in the composition of such assemblies (such as women, youth and racial minorities) receive insufficient attention.

The lack of social representativeness may result in the institutions of government becoming out of tune with public opinion and being seen as an anachronistic defender of the status quo when the national mood demands reform and innovation. This problem may be accentuated by the procedures adopted by legislative bodies: the seniority system used by the American Congress tended to entrench the conservative influence over post-war American domestic affairs and persisted until changes to these procedures were introduced during the 1960s and 1970s. Groups who perceive that their needs are being inadequately catered for by the institutions of government may resort to alternative means of political expression which may have long-term consequences for the authority of such bodies. Some parties have responded to this issue. For example, the British Labour Party introduced internal regulations which were designed to increase the number of women candidates for public office.

THE COMPOSITION OF THE BRITISH HOUSE OF COMMONS

At the 1992 general election 651 Members of Parliament were elected. Of these, 60 (9%) were women, 6 (1%) were from ethnic minority communities. The remainder (90%) were white males.

An all-party campaign, the Three Hundred Group, seeks the election of 300 women to the House of Commons as one of its objectives. The joint proposals of the Scottish Labour Party and Liberal Democrats for a Scottish Parliament include the aim of equal representation of men and women in such an assembly.

Public involvement in policy making

What mechanisms might be used by liberal democratic political systems to enable the general public to be involved in political affairs following an election?

It has been argued that elections play a major role in liberal democratic political systems. They enable the population to select a small group of people who perform the tasks of government. However, the ability to elect representatives and (at a subsequent election) to deliver a verdict on their performance in public office does not give the general public a prominent role in political affairs. In many liberal democracies, therefore, there are mechanisms which seek to provide citizens with a more constant role in policy formulation. In this section we consider some of the ways in which this objective can be achieved.

Membership of pressure groups

We consider the operations of pressure groups more fully in Chapter 5. Such organisations provide the public with opportunities to influence policy makers to adopt their proposals. The existence of pressure groups and the competition which occurs between them is viewed as an indispensable aspect of a pluralist society in which power is dispersed and policy emerges as the result of a process of bargaining and conciliation conducted between groups.

Opinion polls

Opinion polls may be utilised to ascertain public feelings on particular issues. The findings ascertained by polls can then be incorporated into the policy proposals put forward by political parties both in government and opposition. Opinion polls seek to determine the views of the public by putting questions to a small group of people. There are several ways in which such a group might be selected. The two main ways are through the use of a random or a quota sample. The first addresses questions to a segment of the public who are chosen by a method which lacks scientific construction. In Britain, for example, a random sample might consist of every thousandth name on the register of electors in a particular parliamentary constituency. A quota sample, however, seeks to address questions to a group of people whose composition is determined in advance. By this method, questions are directed at a group who are perceived to be a cross-section of the public whose views are being sought. It will attempt, for example, to reflect the overall balance between old and young people, men and women and working and middle-class persons.

Polls are especially prominent in election campaigns. They are used to assess the views of voters on particular issues which enables parties to adjust the emphasis of their campaigns (or the content of their policy) to match the popular mood. They are also employed to investigate the outcome of elections by asking voters who they intend to support. The belief that this activity does not merely indicate public feelings but may actually influence voting behaviour (for example, by creating a bandwagon effect for the party judged by the polls to be in the lead) has prompted countries such as France to ban the publication of poll results close to the actual contest.

HOW ACCURATE ARE OPINION POLLS?

Although opinion polls are widely used, especially during election campaigns, they are not consistently accurate. In 1995 the polls wrongly predicted a major victory for Silvio Berlusconi in the Italian regional elections (which his party lost) and a clear victory for Jacques Chirac in the first round of the French presidential election (in which he was defeated by the Socialist, Lionel Jospin).

There are several reasons which might explain the shortcoming of opinion polls. Some people may refuse to answer the pollsters' questions which may distort the result if such refusals are disproportionately made by one segment of electoral opinion. They rely on those who are questioned telling the truth or subsequently adhering to the opinions which they express to the pollsters. The 'last minute swing' phenomenon suggests that members of the general public may alter their minds and depart from a previously expressed opinion. Polls may also find accuracy difficult when the public is evenly divided on the matter under investigation.

Consultation and participation

Members of the general public may also secure involvement in policy making through mechanisms which allow them to express their views to policy makers on particular issues. Consultation implies the right to be heard. Citizens may be invited to express their opinions on particular matters to which the policy makers listen but are not required to act upon. Participation involves a shift in the relationship between policy makers and the public. Policy making is transformed into a joint exercise involving governors and the governed.

Consultation and participation might be regarded as beneficial to liberal democracies as they permit the policy preferences of the public to be considered or acted upon by public officials. However, the lack of information in the hands of the general public might make meaningful discussion impossible and may even result in the public being manipulated into giving their backing to contentious proposals put forward by the policy makers.

Referendums

What is a referendum and does this provide a desirable way to increase the role of the general public in policy making?

Referendums give the general public the opportunity to vote on specific policy issues. They are utilised widely in some liberal democracies such as Switzerland and the Scandinavian countries but more sparingly in others such as Britain.

Advantages

The main advantages associated with referendums are as follows:

Direct democracy

Referendums facilitate mass public involvement in the formulation of public policy. A proposal requires the sanction of the majority of citizens in order for it to be implemented. The dangers inherent in liberal democracy of public office holders not accurately reflecting public opinion on the disparate array of policy proposals which come before them is avoided through the operations of a system of direct democracy enabling the citizens themselves to express their approval or disapproval of issues which affect their everyday lives. The power exercised by the legislative and executive branches of government over the content of public policy is thus reduced. Governments and parliaments may be forced to pursue actions which are truly reflective of the views of the public rather than leading them in a direction in which the majority do not want to go.

It is important, however, that the initiative to hold a referendum should not solely rest with those who discharge the functions of government. If referendums are to provide a mechanism to facilitate public involvement in policy making it is important that the public themselves should have the right both to call one and to exercise some control over its content. In New Zealand, for example, the 1993 Citizens Initiated Referenda Act gave 10% of registered electors the opportunity to initiate a non-binding referendum on any subject. This must be held within one year of the initial call for a referendum unless 75% of Members of Parliament vote to defer it.

Determination of constitutional issues
It is not feasible to suggest that referendums should be held to judge the mood of the public on every item of public policy. However, they do provide a means whereby major issues (perhaps of considerable constitutional importance) can be resolved. In many European countries referendums were held on membership of the European Union or treaties (such as Maastricht) which were associated with it because of their implications for fundamental matters such as national sovereignty. In Britain, a Referendum Party was established in 1994 calling for a referendum on the European issue which would cover the Maastricht Treaty and its subsequent revisions.

Disadvantages

Devaluing the role of the legislature
Referendums may devalue the role performed by legislative bodies. In some countries (such as France) they were deliberately introduced to weaken the power of parliament. Although one can reconcile them with the concept of Parliamentary sovereignty by viewing them as consultative rather than binding on the actions of the legislature, it is difficult to ignore the outcome of a popular vote even when it does not theoretically tie the hands of public policy makers. Thus the Norwegian Parliament announced in advance of the 1972 consultative referendum on entry into the European Economic Community that its outcome would determine the country's stance on this issue.

Unequal competition
Competing groups in a referendum do not necessarily possess equality in the resources which they have at their disposal and this may give one side an unfair advantage over the other in putting its case across to the electorate. This problem is accentuated if the government contributes to the financing of one side's campaign, as occurred in the early stages of the 1995 Irish referendum on divorce.

Complexity of issues
It has also been argued that the general public is often unable to understand the complexities of the issues which may be addressed to them in a referendum. This may mean that the level of public participation is low or that the result is swayed by factors other than the

issue which is placed before the voters for their consideration. A referendum may be used by the voters to express an opinion on an incumbent government if such has become unpopular and is closely associated with one course of action open to them in such a contest. The outcome of the French referendum in 1969 to re-establish the region as a unit of government was heavily influenced by the unpopularity of President de Gaulle with whom such a proposal was closely identified.

Underlying motives may not be progressive

We should also observe that a referendum is not always a progressive measure designed to enhance the ability of the public to play a meaningful role in policy making. Dictators such as Hitler used referendums as a device to secure popular approval of actions which had already taken place. Referendums may also be proposed by executives as a means to preserve party unity on an issue which is extremely divisive. The British referendum in 1975 on the Labour government's re-negotiated terms for membership of the European Economic Community was primarily put forward for such partisan reasons. This avoided the government having to take a decision which might have split the party. The suggestion that a referendum might be held to determine whether Britain should join a single European currency would serve a similar purpose for the Conservative Party.

'Mob rule'

It is also argued that a referendum may facilitate the tyranny of the majority with minority interests being sacrificed at the behest of mob rule. One danger associated with this objection is that political affairs may be resolved by orchestrated hysteria rather than through a calm reflection of the issues which are involved.

EXAMPLES OF THE USE OF REFERENDUMS

Ireland: Proposals to amend the constitution, following enactment by the *Oireachtas*, (parliament) must be submitted to a referendum. In 1995 a proposal to amend the constitution and legalise divorce was narrowly approved, having been decisively rejected in 1986.

France: Referendums have been initiated by some presidents to appeal directly to the public over the

---

	heads of either the National Assembly or the government. President de Gaulle's 1962 referendum secured popular approval for the direct election of the president and demonstrated how a referendum can be used to enhance presidential power.
Italy:	A number of referendums were held in the 1990s on the issue of electoral reform. They may be initiated by 500,000 electors.

'Teledemocracy'

Referendums are one mechanism of direct democracy. But there are others. What is termed 'teledemocracy' can also be used to achieve the objective of enhanced popular involvement in public policy making. This involves a television audience being supplied with the technology to make an instant response to matters which appear on their screens. Experiments have taken place in countries which include America and New Zealand. Although these have often been concerned with marketing commercial products and entertainment they could be further developed to facilitate members of the general public being regularly involved in the formulation of policy, perhaps through their participation in spontaneous polls concerning options which are debated before them.

The role of the military in civilian affairs

What constraints govern the involvement of the military in civilian affairs in a liberal democracy?

In some areas of the world governments are controlled by members of the military. Government is conducted by soldiers rather than politicians. Nigeria, for example, has been ruled by military governments for most of the period since independence and in 1993 the president, General Ibrahim Babangida, declared the election results void when it appeared that the presidency had been won by an opposition candidate.

In liberal democratic political systems we are likely to view the military as an institution concerned with defending the interests of our country at home or abroad. But we sometimes see soldiers performing duties in our own country too. Such tasks are of a civilian rather than a military nature. Thus we need to consider how the involvement of the military in civilian affairs in liberal democracies differs from that which it performs in oligarchic political structures.

One feature of a liberal democracy is that the military is subject to civilian control. This means that it does not intervene in civil affairs at its own discretion but awaits a request to do so from what is termed a civil authority. This control extends to implementing objectives which are determined by politicians who may subsequently be called upon to account for the actions of the military. In America the president is the commander-in-chief of the armed forces. In Britain the authority which summoned military intervention in civilian affairs was historically a magistrate. Today government ministers and chief constables play key roles in decisions of this kind. There are three circumstances in which military intervention in civil affairs may be justified in contemporary Britain.

These are Military Aid to the Civilian Communities (which covers events such a providing help to the public in the wake of natural disasters such as floods), Military Aid to the Civilian Ministries (in which military aid is sought to provide a service required by the public when such has been withdrawn, for example in a strike) and Military Aid to the Civil Power (when military support is needed to ensure public order). Troops were deployed in Northern Ireland after 1969 under this latter contingency.

Questions

1 List six points which you consider to be the essential characteristics of a liberal democratic political system.
2 'A healthy liberal democracy takes the views of members of the general public into account when formulating policy'. Evaluate two ways in which this objective can be achieved.
3 With reference to any liberal democracy with which you are familiar, assess the extent to which the composition of the legislature reflects the social-composition of the population. Do you consider the lack of social representativeness to be a problem for the operations of liberal democratic political systems?
4 List three arguments in favour of the use of referendums and three against.

Summary

1 Liberal democracy is a political system which seeks to ensure that
   the operations of government reflect the will of the majority of the
   population. Government operates in the name of the people and is
   ultimately accountable to them for its actions.
2 Elections are key mechanisms for ensuring that government
   operates in accordance with popular sentiments. But the use of
   elections is not confined to liberal democracies. In such political
   systems they need to be underpinned by a number of essential
   political freedoms which include:
   ● the regular holding of elections
   ● the freedom of political expression and activity and freedom
     from arbitrary arrest
   ● a wide suffrage
   ● citizens should be free from intimidation or coercion when
     casting their votes.
3 The extent to which members of the executive and legislative
   branches of government represent popular opinion is subject to a
   number of considerations. These include:
   ● the strength of the party system
   ● the operations of the electoral system
   ● the status of elected officials, who may be either representatives
     or delegates
   ● the extent to which the legislature in particular is socially
     representative of the general population.
4 Elections confine the role of the general public to choosing
   members of the legislative and executive branches of government.
   In many liberal democratic political systems the public are also
   enabled to play a more active role in policy formulation. They may
   do this by joining pressure groups and through mechanisms
   (including opinion polls) which seek to provide for public consultation
   or participation. Some liberal democracies make use of referendums
   to enhance the role of the public in policy making.
5 In a liberal democracy the involvement of the military in civil
   affairs is subject to civilian control and the military does not
   intervene at its own discretion.

3

ELECTIONS AND ELECTORAL SYSTEMS

The significance of elections

What is the purpose of elections?

Those of us who live in liberal democracies will periodically be invited to vote. We may be asked to choose representatives for local, state or national office. Elections, therefore, are a key mechanism in which the citizens of a liberal democracy are given the opportunity to play some part in the political affairs of their country. They facilitate public participation in key activities which include the choice of candidates for public office and the content of public policy.

Elections further constitute the process whereby public office holders can be made to account for their activities to the general public. It is an essential feature of liberal democracy that sovereignty resides with the people living in each country. Governments must be accountable to the people for their actions. Those which lose the backing of public opinion will be replaced by representatives drawn from another political party at the next round of elections. Elections, therefore, provide an essential link between the government and the governed. They serve as a barometer of public opinion and ensure that the holders of public office, and the policies which they pursue, are broadly in accord with the wishes of the general public.

Non-voting

What factors might explain why electors do not vote? Are low levels of voter participation a problem for liberal democracies?

It is sometimes argued that the extent to which citizens exercise their right to vote is one indicator of the 'health' of that system of government. A high level of voter participation (which is sometimes referred to as 'turnout') might suggest enthusiasm by members of the public to involve themselves in the affairs of government in their country and in more general terms, to express support for the political system which operates in that country.

In some liberal democracies voting is compulsory: this is the case in Australia and Belgium, for example. In others, however, it is optional.

Where voting is optional, the level of voter participation varies. In 1992 the turnout for the British general election was 77.8%. In the same year only 55.9% of the American public voted in the presidential election.

Various reasons might explain non-voting. Factors such as social class, education and income may be influential forces in determining whether a person votes or abstains. Generally, low voting rates are found among persons from low socio-economic backgrounds. Voting laws and registration procedures may also influence turnout. In Britain, for example, local authorities actively seek to ensure that voters are registered. In America, the onus of registration is placed upon the individual.

There is debate as to the significance of low levels of voting. It might be argued that low turnouts result in public policy failing to represent the national interest. If public opinion is imperfectly represented, governments may be swayed to act at the behest of organised minorities. Lack of popular involvement in the affairs of government may further pave the way for authoritarianism in which the public are effectively frozen out of participation in government. Alternatively, however, it might be argued that low voting levels are not of great importance. Non-voting may indicate a general level of popular satisfaction with the way in which public affairs are conducted.

The mandate

We often hear governments justify their actions by the claim that they have a mandate to carry out such actions. What does this mean?

Candidates for public office are usually selected by political parties. To contest elections, they generally put forward a statement of the principles or policies which will guide their future actions if they succeed in taking control of public affairs. In Britain such a statement is termed an election manifesto. A party which succeeds in gaining control of a public body through the election of its nominees claims to have a mandate to administer it in line with the statements contained in its election manifesto. Its right to do this has been legitimised by the process of popular election.

THE INFLUENCE OF THE MANDATE

How important is the concept of the mandate?

In some Liberal democracies such as Britain, it is influential. It forces a political party to declare the policies which will determine its subsequent actions if it gains control of a public authority. But it can also claim the right to carry out such policies on the grounds that the public has endorsed them.

In other countries, this concept may be of less importance. In America, for example, voters are heavily influenced by the previous record of incumbent candidates There is some tendency to look back and cast votes retrospectively rather than seeking to evaluate the merits of proposed future actions by candidates and parties. Nonetheless, candidates for public office usually put forward a statement of future intentions. Candidates for the presidency announce their platform at the nominating convention.

There are, however, several weaknesses associated with the concept of the mandate. This may lead us to conclude that while it is useful in a liberal democracy that parties should declare their policies to the voters at election time it is unrealistic to expect that statements such as those contained in election manifestos can give a thorough and complete guide to what a party will do when in control of a public authority. It is also inaccurate for a winning party to assert that the public has demonstrated support for the entire contents of its manifesto. The main problems associated with the mandate are amplified below.

The emergence of issues following an election

It would be unrealistic for us to expect that a party could include every item of policy which it intended to carry out over a period of several years in a single document prepared for a specific election. Issues emerge, unforeseen when the manifesto was prepared, which have to be responded to even though the public lacks the opportunity to express their views on them. British people, for example, were not invited to vote on the despatch of a task force to recapture the Falkland Islands in 1982 nor whether they wanted to commit British troops to the Gulf in 1990.

We accept, therefore, that once installed into office governments need to exercise a certain amount of discretion to respond to pressing problems when they arise. This capacity to act without consulting the general public is referred to as trusteeship.

Voters endorse parties rather than their policies

A party's right to carry out all of its promises on the grounds that the public expressed support for them is also a flawed argument. Electors are unable to pick and choose between those policies in a manifesto which they like and those which they disapprove of. It is a question of supporting all or nothing. It is also the case that voters support a party for reasons other than the policies which it advances. Factors such as social class may determine a voter's political allegiance. In extreme circumstances this may mean that parties secure support in spite of, rather than because of, the policies they put forward.

Voting may be influenced by negative factors

A party or its candidates may secure support for negative rather than positive reasons. It was argued that the 1992 American presidential election was primarily a referendum on the presidency of George Bush, especially his handling of the economy. Many voters supported Bill Clinton and Ross Perot because they were dissatisfied with President Bush. Such negative support makes it difficult for parties and their candidates to claim they have a mandate to carry out their policies.

The first-past-the-post system and its variants

How does the first-past-the-post electoral system operate?

The first-past-the-post system is used in countries which include Britain, the United States, Canada and India.

Under this system to be elected to a public office it is necessary for a candidate to secure more votes than the person who comes second. But there is no requirement that the winning candidate should secure an overall majority of the votes cast in an election. It is thus possible for a candidate to be victorious under this system despite having secured a minority of the votes cast in an election.

THE FIRST-PAST-THE-POST SYSTEM – AN EXAMPLE

Let us consider an example of the manner in which the first-past-the-post electoral system operates.

In the Scottish Parliamentary constituency of Argyll and Bute at the 1992 general election the following result was obtained:

Liberal Democrat	12,739
Conservative	10,117
SNP	8,689
Labour	4,946

The Liberal Democrat candidate was returned although she obtained only 34.9% of the vote cast in that constituency.

Elsewhere systems of election have been devised which seek to adjust the workings of the first-past-the-post system. These are the second ballot and the alternative vote. Neither of these constitute systems of proportional representation although they do attempt to ameliorate some of the injustices which may arise under the first-past-the-post system.

The second ballot

The second ballot is used in France both for legislative and presidential elections. The process is a two-stage affair. It is necessary for a candidate to obtain an overall majority of votes cast in the first-round election in order to secure election to public office. In other words, if 50,000 people voted in a constituency it would be necessary for a candidate to secure 25,001 votes to be elected. If no candidate obtained this required figure, a second-round election is held in which the candidate with most votes is elected. This system seeks to ensure that the winning candidate gets the endorsement of a majority of the electors who cast their votes in the second election.

For presidential contests the second ballot is between the top two candidates from the first round. In 1995 the second-round contest was between Lionel Jospin and Jacques Chirac with the seven other first-round candidates eliminated. For elections to the National Assembly, any candidate who obtains 12.5% of the vote in the first-round may enter the second ballot. In practice, however, parties of the left and right have often agreed in advance to rally behind one candidate for the second ballot.

The alternative vote

The alternative vote is used in Ireland for presidential elections and for by-elections to the lower house, the *Dáil*. It is also used to select members for the Australian House of Representatives. As with the second ballot a candidate cannot be elected without obtaining majority support from the electorate (namely 50% + 1 of the votes cast). Unlike the second ballot, however, there is no second election.

Voters number candidates in order of preference. If, when these votes are counted, no candidate possesses an overall majority, the candidate with least first-preference votes is eliminated and these are redistributed to the candidate placed second on that candidate's ballot paper. This process is repeated until a candidate has an overall majority composed of his or her first-preference votes coupled with the redistributed votes of candidates who have been eliminated.

Proportional representation

What is the objective of proportional representation and how might this be achieved?

Proportional representation indicates an objective rather than a specific method of election. It seeks to guarantee that the wishes of the electorate are arithmetically reflected in the composition of public authorities. This is achieved by ensuring that parties are represented on public bodies according to the level of popular support they enjoy at an election contest. Various forms of proportional representation are used widely in countries which comprise the European Union.

This section will consider two of these – the single transferable vote and the party list system. Both of these methods of election constitute systems of proportional representation.

The single transferable vote

The single transferable vote applies to elections to legislative bodies. It requires an area to be divided into a number of multi-member constituencies (that is, constituencies which return more than one member to the legislative body). When electors cast their votes, they are required to number candidates in order of preference. They may indicate a preference for as many, or as few, candidates as they wish. To be elected, a candidate has to secure a quota of votes.

THE 'DROOP QUOTA'

Under the single transferable vote a candidate is required to secure a quota of votes in order to be elected. This quota (which is termed the 'droop quota', after its nineteenth century 'inventor', Henry Droop) is calculated by the following formula:

$$\left(\frac{\text{Total number of votes cast in the constituency}}{\text{Total number of seats to be filled}} \right) + 1$$

Thus in a constituency in which 100,000 electors voted and in which there were four seats to be filled, the quota would be 20,001. Any candidate who obtains the necessary number of first-preference votes is declared elected. Further first-preference votes cast for that candidate are then redistributed to the candidates listed second on that candidate's ballot paper.

If, when the count is complete, no candidate obtains the necessary number of first-preference votes, the candidate with fewest is eliminated and these are redistributed to the candidates listed as second choice on the eliminated candidate's ballot paper. This process of eliminating candidates with fewest first-preference votes is continued until the requisite number of seats are filled.

The single transferable vote system ensures that each successful candidate is elected by the same number of votes. It is used in Ireland for elections to the *Dáil* and for the majority of seats in the upper chamber (the *Seanad*). 49 of the 60 members, are elected in this fashion. This system is employed in Malta and in Northern Ireland for the election of Members of the European Parliament.

The party list system

The other main system of proportional representation is the party list system. A main objective of this system is to ensure that parties are represented in legislative bodies in proportion to the votes which were cast for them. Political parties are responsible for drawing up lists of candidates which may be compiled on a national or on a regional basis. In South Africa 200 members of the National Assembly are elected from regional party lists and the other 200 from national lists.

These candidates are put forward by the party in order of preference. When the votes are counted a party's representation in the legislative body arithmetically reflects the proportion of votes which it obtained. In a very simplistic form (in what is termed a 'closed party list') a party which obtained 20 per cent of the total national poll would be entitled to 20 per cent of the seats in the legislative chamber. If this chamber contained 300 members, this party would be entitled to fill 60 places. The actual nominees would be those numbered 1–60 on that party's list.

There are several varieties of party list systems. A popular one in Europe is the *D'Hondt* system which is used for national elections in Belgium, the Netherlands, Portugal and Spain. Under this system it is possible for electors to vote for specific candidates selected from the lists drawn up by the parties. This enables the voters to indicate their views on the standing of candidates put forward by a political party. In this case what is termed the 'highest average' formula seeks to ensure that approximately the same number of votes are required to elect candidates drawn from the same political party.

There are several variations of this system including the *hagenbach-bischoff* system which is used in elections to the Greek Parliament and the *panochage* system which is used for elections to the Luxembourg Parliament. A particular feature of the latter system is the 'mix-in' whereby voters are not confined to selecting candidates from one party's list but may support candidates nominated by different parties. This is termed a 'free party list'.

The additional member system

There are also hybrid systems which seek to blend the first-past-the-post system with proportional representation. In Germany, for example, both systems are used concurrently in order that minority parties who fare badly under the former system can be compensated under the latter. Under this country's additional member system, electors have two votes in parliamentary elections. The first (*erststimme*) is for a constituency candidate, elected under the first-past-the-post system. The second (*zweitstimme*) is for a party list drawn up in each state (or *Länder*). The Niedermeyer system is used to allocate additional members according to the following formula:

$$\frac{\text{Total votes obtained by a party} \times \text{number of seats available}}{\text{Total number of votes of all parties getting above 5\%}}$$

The latter serves as a 'top up' seeking to ensure that there is a degree of proportionality between the parties. This system gives electors the opportunity of 'split ticket' voting: that is they can support a constituency candidate of one party and the party list of another. This is a growing feature in German elections.

Elections to the lower house of the Russian Parliament, the *Duma*, in 1995 utilised a mixed system of first-past-the-post and proportional representation by the party list system. In 1993 a referendum in New Zealand narrowly supported changing the electoral system from first-past-the-post to a mixed member system, whose main features are similar to the electoral system used in Germany. This will come into force for the next general election, scheduled to be held in 1996.

The first-past-the-post electoral system analysed

What are the main strengths and weaknesses of the first-past-the-post electoral system?

Strengths

Easy to understand
The system is relatively easy to understand. Voting is a simple process and it is easy to see how the result is arrived at. The winner takes all.

Executive strength
There is a distortion in this system which tends to benefit the party winning most votes. Although this may operate against minority parties, it provides the executive with an aura of strength. The authority of the executive to govern is thereby enhanced.

An aid to party unity
The manner in which this system treats minorities may serve as an inducement for parties either to remain united or to form electoral alliances in order to secure political power. This may be an advantage in those countries where the executive is drawn from the legislative body. Support for the government within the legislature is likely to be durable.

Enhancement of the link between the citizens and legislators
The first-past-the-post system may strengthen the relationship between members of the legislative branch of government and their constituents. In Britain the House of Commons is composed of Members elected from 651 single-member constituencies which facilitates a close relationship developing between individual legislators and their constituents. This may also enhance the extent to which legislators can be held accountable for their actions. Such local relationships are also of great significance to the conduct of American politics.

'STRONG GOVERNMENT' IN BRITAIN AND AMERICA

The winner takes all aspect of the first-past-the-post system is greatly to the benefit of the executive branch of government. This is regardless of whether this branch is drawn from the legislature (as it is in Britain) or is separately elected (as in America).

In the 1992 general election in Great Britain a Conservative government was returned for a fourth term. Although this party obtained only 41.9% of the votes cast by the electorate, the workings of the first-past-the-post system gave it an overall majority of 21 in the House of Commons (51.6% of the seats). This majority, although a reduced figure from that obtained in the previous election, should have been sufficient to enable the government to pursue its policies and govern for a reasonable period of time.

In the 1992 presidential election in the United States, President Clinton defeated the incumbent President Bush but obtained only 43% of the popular votes cast. However, the electoral college vote for each state was allocated on the winner-takes-all principle of the first-past-the-post system. Accordingly, President Clinton obtained 370 votes to Mr Bush's 168. This gave the former an aura of political strength.

Weaknesses

Distortion of public opinion
It has been suggested that the purpose of elections is to ensure that public office holders and the policies they pursue are reflective of public opinion. A main problem with the first-past-the-post system is that it distorts public opinion by failing to ensure that the wishes of the electorate are arithmetically reflected in the composition of the legislative or executive branches of government. This may thus result in public policy being out of line with the views or wishes of the majority of the general public.

There are two further aspects to this distortion of public opinion. First, the first-past-the-post system is capable of producing extreme changes in the composition of the legislative and executive branches of government which does not absolutely reflect the feelings of the electorate. Major political parties can be virtually wiped out by such a system. An extreme example of this occurred in the 1993 Canadian general election when the ruling Conservative Party was reduced from 157 seats to 2. Violent changes in the composition of the legislature or executive may also result in the loss of experienced personnel and may create a system of adversarial politics.

Unfair treatment of minority parties
A second issue arising from the operations of the first-past-the-post system is the manner in which it treats minority parties. British Liberal Democrats campaign for electoral reform on the grounds that their parliamentary strength is a gross distortion of their popular appeal. The electoral system fails to translate that party's votes into seats within the legislature. The Liberal Democrats suffer from the fact that their support is relatively evenly spread across the country and between the social classes. But they rarely possess the capacity to secure victory in individual parliamentary constituencies.

Thus in the 1992 general election the Liberal Democrats secured 17.9% of the total vote yet secured only 3% of the seats in the House of Commons. Had the electoral system reflected the views of the electorate, the party would have secured 117 seats rather than the 20 it succeeded in winning. Expressing this figures another way, in 1992:

It took   41,957   votes to elect a Conservative MP
It took   42,646   votes to elect a Labour MP
It took 299,735   votes to elect a Liberal Democrat MP

which contravenes the principle of 'one vote, one value'.

The Scottish National Party was equally adversely treated at this election, securing 21.5% of the total vote in Scotland but returning only three MPs. Similarly, Ross Perot's strong showing in the 1992 American presidential election failed to secure him a single vote in the electoral college.

ELECTORAL REFORM IN BRITAIN

Traditionally the case for electoral reform in Britain has been voiced by vested interests. A belief by a political party that the electoral system is working against their interests but to the benefit of their opponents has frequently prompted calls for reform.

Britain's major parties have been willing to contemplate reform when it suited them. The dominance of the Conservative Party after 1979 was one reason why some members of the Labour Party began to display an interest in this subject. However, the most consistent demands for electoral reform have come from the Liberal Party/Liberal Democrats.

In more recent years, however, the debate has begun to move away from vested interests and towards a view of electoral reform as a mechanism to develop a new relationship between government and the governed. Many in the Labour Party now view such a reform (in association with others such as the referendum) as a necessary step to bring government and the people closer together.

Discouragement to voter participation
A further problem with the first-past-the-post system is that it may discourage voter participation. Areas may be considered 'safe' political territory for one party or another and this may discourage opponents of that party from voting on the grounds that if they do so their vote is effectively 'wasted'.

The downplaying of ideology

It has been argued that the first-past-the-post system tends to discourage parties from fragmenting and thus to promote the conduct of politics within the confines of a two-party system. However, this may result in ideology becoming diluted, obscured or played down in order for the parties to serve as vehicles capable of attracting a wide range of political opinions. The absence of a distinct identity may result in voters becoming disinterested in the conduct of politics. The consequence of this is low turnouts in elections and the utilisation of alternative ways (such as pressure group activity) in order to bring about political change.

The attainment of the benefits of the first-past-the-post system

We must finally analyse some of the stated advantages of the first-past-the-post system and consider whether these are necessarily helpful to the conduct of politics and the extent to which these theoretical benefits are actually realised in practice. To do this we shall examine the situation in Britain.

In Britain the executive branch of government comes from the majority party in the legislative body. However, strong governments (in the sense of the executive having a large parliamentary majority and thus being in a position to ensure the enactment of its election manifesto) have not been a consistent feature of post-war politics. Fourteen general elections have been held between 1945 and 1992: in six of these (1950, 1951, 1964, February 1974, October 1974 and 1992) governments were returned with a relatively small (and in one case – February 1974 – no) overall majority in the House of Commons. Governments in this position cannot guarantee to stay in office and carry out their policies. On one occasion (between 1977 and 1978) the Labour and Liberal Parliamentary parties concluded a pact which had the effect of sustaining what had become a minority Labour government. Thus the first-past-the-post electoral system does not always deliver the benefits which advocates claim this system possesses.

The strengths and weaknesses of proportional representation

Is it correct to argue that the disadvantages of proportional representation outweigh its advantages?

Advantages

The main advantage of proportional representation is that the system addresses many of the defects of the first-past-the-post system. It ensures that minorities are fairly treated. Legislative bodies throughout Europe contain members drawn from parties such as the Greens and thus provide an inducement for these groups to operate within the conventional political system. Such an inducement is absent in Britain where the poll obtained by that party in the 1989 European elections (15%) failed to secure the return of any members to the European Parliament. Proportional representation may also induce parties to co-operate (especially in cases where the executive is drawn from the legislative body) and this may, in turn, divert politics away from extremes.

Disadvantages

Let us first consider the following example. In 1986, President Mitterrand of France introduced proportional representation (in the form of the party list system) for the French legislative elections in order to dilute the strength of the dominant conservative forces in the country (the RPR and the UDF) One consequence of this was the election of a number of representatives from the *Front national*. This party obtained 10% of the vote and secured 35 seats. In 1988 the second ballot was restored by the prime minister, Jacques Chirac, and the *Front national* was virtually eliminated as a legislative force. This episode illustrates two problems which might be associated with proportional representation which are discussed below.

Furtherance of vested interests

First we should note the association of this reform with political vested interests in this example – it was not viewed as a progressive reform which would improve the relationship between government and the governed.

Representation given to political extremists
Secondly, this example suggests that proportional representation may facilitate the representation of the political extremes which, once established within a legislative body, gain respectability and may enjoy a growth in their support. Some countries which use this system seek to guard against this problem by imposing a requirement that a party needs to secure a minimum threshold of support in order to secure any representation. In Denmark this figure is 2% and in Germany, 5% (although a variation was introduced for the 1990 and 1994 elections).

There are other problems associated with proportional representation.

Multiparty systems
The encouragement which proportional representation provides for political extremes is symptomatic of a more general problem which is that this system may promote the development of a multiparty system. This is of particular significance for those countries whose executives are drawn from the legislative body. In these cases, multiparty systems may make it difficult either to select the personnel of the executive or to determine what policies should be enacted. Executives may consist of a coalition of parties which are often depicted as being weak and unstable.

PROPORTIONAL REPRESENTATION AND MINOR PARTIES

Those who object to proportional representation assert that minor parties might secure a role in a country's political affairs which is out of all proportion to their levels of support. The German Free Democratic Party has enjoyed participation in government since 1969 as for many years it held a pivotal position between Christian Democrats and the Social Democrats. It could keep either out of office by siding with the other. It has managed to retain its place in government despite its declining level of support which led to the resignation of its leader, Klaus Kinkel, in 1995.

Complexity
Critics of proportional representation also argue that the system is difficult in the sense that it may not be obvious how the eventual

result has been arrived at. This is especially the case with the single transferable vote which requires a process of redistribution (either of the surplus votes of an elected candidate or of the redundant votes of one who has been eliminated). Such votes are not randomly redistributed and electors may not fully understand the manner by which this process is carried out. A danger with this is that if the process by which the result is arrived at is not fully understood, the result itself may be deprived of popular legitimacy.

Enhancement of position of party leadership
Proportional representation has been accused of enhancing the power of the party leadership. This is especially the case with the party list system which gives regional or national party leaders the ability to place candidates in order of preference and thereby improve the chances of loyal party members being elected ahead of those who are regarded as dissentients. This objection is, however, mitigated by the ability of electors to vote for individual candidates in many countries which utilise the party list method of election.

Impact on legislator and constituent relationships
It might be argued that proportional representation weakens the link between legislator and constituent which in countries such as Britain and America is regarded as a crucial political feature. But this is not necessarily the case. The multimember constituencies used for elections to the *Dáil* in Ireland are small: 41 constituencies returning 166 members. There are at least three MPs to each constituency whose average population is between 20,000 and 30,000. The ability of electors to express support for individual candidates under some versions of the party list system may also serve to enhance the relationship between constituent and representative.

Coalition government assessed

Proportional representation does not necessarily result in a multiparty system. The single transferable vote did not prevent the dominance of *Fianna Fáil* over Irish government for many years. Nor (as we will discover in Chapter 4) should we uncritically accept the argument that proportional representation is the cause of multiparty systems. However, below we analyse whether coalition governments are an undesirable political phenomenon.

Absence of popular choice

It might be argued that the formation of a coalition government and the determination of the policies which it will pursue are not conducted in a democratic manner. Although separate political parties can enter into pacts or alliances prior to an election contest, coalition governments are frequently formed after an election has taken place allowing party leaders to conduct negotiations. These discussions may be lengthy and drawn out and the electorate is not consulted concerning the composition of the executive or the choice of policy it pursues.

Ineffective accountability

It is also argued that accountability is impaired by coalition governments. When several parties are involved in government it may be difficult for the electorate to make any single party answer for its actions.

Instability

Coalition governments are also accused of being unwieldy. A minor party may desert the government and the whole structure tumbles down. The downfall of the Berlusconi government in 1994 (due to the desertion of the Northern League – the *Lega Nord*) and the downfall of the Reynolds government in Ireland in the same year (following the desertion of the Irish Labour Party) are examples which can be used to justify the argument that coalition governments are unstable. Italy has had in excess of 50 post-war governments. Such difficulties were one consideration which prompted Italian voters to move away from proportional representation. Following a referendum to end proportional representation for elections to the Senate in 1993, new election rules were introduced under which 75 per cent of the seats in a general election were subject to the first-past-the-post system of election. The remaining seats were allocated by proportional representation.

We should observe, however, that coalition governments are not inevitably weak and unstable. A coalition of the Christian Democrats, the Christian-Social Union and the Free Democrats have provided Germany's government since 1982. It was confirmed in office in the 1990 'all-German' election and held onto power in the 1994 *Bundestag* elections. The existence of local authorities in Britain in which no single party possesses an overall majority (termed 'hung councils') has in some cases forced political parties to co-operate and may help legitimate coalition government in a country in which this has previously only been resorted to in times of emergency (1931 and 1940).

Questions

1 What do you consider to be the main roles performed by elections in liberal democratic systems of government?
2 'Governments should only pursue those policies for which they obtained a mandate at the previous election'. List points in support and opposition to this statement.
3 Based on the evidence contained in this chapter, do you think that the benefits of the first-past-the-post system are outweighed by its disadvantages?
4 Using sources such as newspapers, textbooks and journals, make a study of one country which uses a system of proportional representation. Based on this study, indicate the main strengths and weaknesses of this system for the conduct of government in that country.

Summary

1 Elections are a means whereby the general public exercises choice over candidates for public office and the content of public policy. They also serve as a mechanism to provide for the accountability of public office holders to those who elected them.
2 The extent to which citizens vote in elections varies. Voter participation is influenced by factors which include social class, education and income. In America the registration procedure may also affect turnout.
3 In many liberal democracies, the concept of the mandate is important. This means that a party which gains control of a public body can claim the right to carry out its policies in accordance with the statements contained in its election programme. But there are weaknesses to this concept. A government may be expected to use its discretion to handle issues which unexpectedly arise after an election and support for a party does not necessarily imply widespread public approval of all of its policies. Parties may secure support for negative rather than positive reasons.
4 A variety of methods are used by liberal democracies to elect candidates for public office. However, a basic division occurs between the first-past-the-post system and proportional representation. There are variants of both of these systems and countries such as Germany and Russia utilise both in their legislative elections.

5 The first-past-the-post system possesses a number of strengths. The system is an easy one to understand, it tends to provide strong government and promotes a close relationship between public office holders and their constituents. However, there are weaknesses associated with this system. In particular the composition of the legislative branch of government does not mirror the votes cast by the electorate and is traditionally unfair to minority parties.

6 Proportional representation remedies many of the weaknesses of the first-past-the-post electoral system: in particular, minorities are more fairly treated. But there are some disadvantages associated with this method of election. It may enable extremist groups to secure representation in legislative assemblies or facilitate multiparty systems and coalition governments, which are often depicted as being weak and unstable. Some systems of proportional representation (such as the party list system) may enhance the power of a party's leadership.

4

PARTIES AND
PARTY SYSTEMS

Objectives and key characteristics

What are the main features of political parties in liberal democratic political systems?

We are familiar with political parties. They are especially prominent at election times. But what do they do?

The main aim of a political party is to secure power by exercising control over government. Its key objectives are to determine the composition of the personnel composing the national government and the policies which it carries out, although parties also operate at state and local levels. To achieve these objectives a party may operate independently or it can co-operate with other political parties.

We tend to regard political parties openly competing for power as the hallmark of a liberal democracy. However political parties often exist in countries which do not possess a liberal democratic political system. The ability to inaugurate meaningful change within society is thus an important qualification required by political parties in a liberal democracy. They should be able to carry out their policies without hindrance from other state institutions.

DOMINANT PARTY SYSTEMS AND ONE-PARTY STATES

We might believe that it is essential in a liberal democracy that office should alternate between political parties. However, in some countries one party frequently wins national elections. This was so for *Fianna Fáil* (which held office in Ireland for 37 of the 43 years between 1932 and 1973), and for the British Conservative Party which won each general election held between 1979 and 1992. In Germany Dr Helmut Kohl's Christian Socialist-dominated government has been in power since 1982.

However, in all of these countries the replacement of the party holding office is theoretically possible and it is the potential of change which separates a one-party state from one in which a single political party is dominant but which could be replaced through the process of free elections.

A party possesses a formal structure which involves national leadership and local organisation. The main role of the latter is to contest elections and recruit party members. This organisation is permanent although it may be most active at election times. The relationship between a party's leaders and its membership varies quite considerably, especially the extent to which a party's leaders can be held accountable for their actions by its rank-and-file supporters. Policy making is frequently the preserve of the party's national leadership which may also possess some degree of control over the selection of candidates for public office.

FACTIONS AND TENDENCIES

Pressure groups are sometimes found within political parties. There is a basic division between a faction and a tendency.

A faction is a group with organisation and a reasonably stable membership. It may be viewed as 'a party within a party'. The Italian Christian Democrats, for example, are sometimes described as a coalition of several factions.

A tendency consists of people within a party who share common opinions but which does not possess formal organisation. The 'Thatcherites' within the contemporary British Conservative Party is an example of a tendency.

Ideology

A political party is usually guided by a political ideology. Its members are thus inspired by a vision of a society which they wish to create in the country where they operate. Ideology thus serves as a unifying force between party leaders and supporters: all are spiritually united in the promotion of a common cause.

Ideology is not, however, always an obvious guiding force in party politics. American political parties appear far less ideological than their western European counterparts. Even in these countries, however, parties (especially when in power) are often forced to respond to events rather than to fashion them and may also be tempted to downplay ideology if they feel this will have a detrimental effect on their level of popular support. Parties on the left of the political spectrum have sometimes been accused of abandoning ideology in favour of pragmatism or of redefining their ideology to make them more electable.

If political ideology is not prominent as a driving force motivating a political party there is a danger that politicians are perceived as seeking office for the power which it gives them as individuals. This may influence the extent of popular involvement in political parties. The absence of pronounced ideology may also result in a situation in which electors find it difficult to differentiate between the political parties. The term 'consensus' is used to describe a situation in which similar goals and policies are espoused by competing political parties. It is argued, for example, that consensus politics dominated British political affairs between 1945 and 1979 and that changes in the internal operations, policies and ultimately, ideology, of the Labour Party illustrated the emergence of a new consensus derived from the electoral successes of the Conservative Party after 1979.

One danger with such a situation (which has allegedly occurred in other industrially developed nations) is that citizens become disenchanted with the main political parties whose dispute largely becomes centred on which can manage the existing economic, social and political system most effectively. This may pave the way for the emergence of extremist political parties (who seem to offer something different) or may underpin the growth of extra-parliamentary political activity as a mechanism to bring about political change.

THE POLITICAL SPECTRUM

The terms 'Left', 'Right' and 'Centre' are frequently used to classify political parties and ideologies. These terms lack precise definition but broadly indicate stances adopted towards political, economic and social change: historically, the Right opposed it, the Left advocated it while the Centre was associated with the desire to introduce gradual reforms to such areas. Conservatism is identified with the right of the spectrum, socialism with the left while liberalism and social democracy is commonly depicted as occupying the centre ground.

The role of political parties

What advantages do political parties bring to the workings of liberal democratic political systems?

Political parties perform a number of roles. In this section we consider the major functions which they fulfil and explain their importance to liberal democratic political structures.

VIEWS OF PARTY

Political parties are now an accepted way for political affairs within liberal democracies to be conducted. But political parties have not always been accepted as helpful political mechanisms.

The American constitution contained no provisions for party government and in his farewell address to the nation in 1796 President Washington bemoaned the 'baneful effects of the spirit of party'. In France, the development of political parties was retarded by a view that they tended to subvert the national interest.

However, in both countries parties are now an accepted feature of political life. The constitution of the fifth French Republic specifically acknowledges their existence.

Selection of candidates and political leaders

Parties are responsible for recruiting and selecting candidates for public office at all levels in the machinery of government. Having selected a candidate, the role of the party is then to secure electoral support for its standard bearer. In particular a country's national leaders emerge through the structure of political parties. Parties provide the main method for selecting a nation's political elite.

This function is an important one. In the nineteenth century monarchs frequently exercised their powers of patronage to select ministers. But with the gradual extension of the right to vote, the composition of governments became the subject of popular choice. The electorate now decided this issue, and its choice was facilitated by the development of party.

THE SELECTION OF CANDIDATES

There are a variety of procedures which parties might use to select candidates.

The choice might be made by the rank and file supporters of a political party. The American system of primary elections opens the choice of candidate to a wide electorate. These elections enable all registered party supporters to select candidates for public office.

Elsewhere, party activists at local level might choose candidates, possibly subject to the approval of the central organs of that party. This is a more restricted electorate, being confined to party members. Such is the practice in Britain in which a key role is played by the constituency organisations in the selection of candidates for local and parliamentary elections.

Finally, the central party organisation might select candidates, perhaps taking local views into consideration. The party list electoral system may encourage the selection of candidates to be made in this fashion.

Organisation of support for national governments

Parties ensure that governments are provided with organised support. This is especially important in systems in which the executive is drawn from the legislative branch of government. In Britain the party whip system in the House of Commons ensures that governments have the necessary backing to implement their policies. The whip consists of written instructions indicating how the party leadership wishes its members to vote. Members who disobey such instructions may have the whip withdrawn. This entails expulsion from their parliamentary party and their replacement with an alternative party candidate at the next election. Without the support of party and its accompanying system of party discipline, governments would be subject to the constant fear of defeat. Such organisation also affects the workings of the opposition parties who are thus able to step in to form a government should the incumbent party be defeated.

However, while parties do aid the operations of liberal democratic political systems, they are not indispensable to it. In America, for example, candidates for public office often promote themselves through personal organisations, even if they latterly attach themselves to a political party. Nor is membership of a major political party essential for those seeking national office. In the 1992 presidential election an independent candidate, Ross Perot, secured 19.7 million votes. This showed that many Americans were willing to endorse as that country's leader a person who had no association with either of the major political parties.

Further, although governments usually rely on the organised support afforded by a political party (or a combination of parties) there are exceptions to this. In 1995 the Italian President, Oscar Luigi Scalfaro, appointed a banker, Lamberto Dini, to be prime minister and head a non-party government. Although this government was seen as a temporary, stop-gap expedient it does illustrate that governments can be formed without the initial backing of established political parties. It possessed sufficient vitality to survive a vote of 'no confidence' in October 1995 designed to force an early general election. Prime Minister Dini resigned at the end of that year and subsequently headed a caretaker administration.

Stimulation of popular interest and involvement in political affairs

Political parties are also beneficial to liberal democracies because they stimulate popular interest and facilitate public participation in political affairs. They perform this function in a number of ways.

Parties need to mobilise the electorate in order to win votes and secure the election of their representatives to public office. This requires the party 'selling' itself to the general public. In theory therefore, a party puts forward its policies and seeks to convince the electorate that these are preferable to those of its opponents. In assessing the arguments which all parties put forward, the electorate thus becomes better informed concerning political affairs.

Second, parties enable persons other than a small elite group of party leaders to be involved in political activity. Members of the general public can join political parties and engage in matters such as candidate selection and policy formulation.

Crucially, parties are a mechanism whereby those who hold public office can be made accountable for their actions. Although elections provide the ultimate means to secure the accountability of public office holders, parties may subject these officials to a more regular, day-by-day scrutiny.

Promoting national harmony

Political parties tend to simplify the conduct of political affairs and make them more manageable. They transform the demands which are made by individuals and groups into programmes which can be put before the electorate. This is known as the 'aggregation of interests' which involves a process of arbitration in which diverse demands are given a degree of coherence by being incorporated into a party platform or manifesto. One consequence of this is to transform parties into 'broad churches' who seek to maximise their level of support by incorporating the claims of a wide cross-section of society.

Such activity may enable parties to promote national harmony. Numerous divisions exist within societies. Such may be based upon class, religion or race. But to win elections, parties have to appeal to as many voters as possible. In doing this they may endorse policies and address appeals which transcend social divisions. Thus parties might serve as a source of national unity. For example, the British Labour Party needs to secure support from a sizeable section of the middle class in order to form a government. Thus it may put forward policies to appeal to such voters. In doing so it bridges the gulf between the working class (whose interests it was formed to advance) and the middle class. One political party thus becomes the vehicle to further the claims of two distinct groups in society.

Providers of patronage

Finally, political parties serve as important sources of patronage. They are able to dispense privileges to their members. The party in charge of the national government is in the best position to do this. The chief executive can make ministerial appointments and thus the party becomes the vehicle through which political ambitions can be realised. Party supporters can also be rewarded. In Britain this includes paid appointments to public bodies and the bestowal of a range of awards through the honours system.

Problems associated with political parties

To what extent are the benefits associated with political parties consistently realised in practice?

Relationship between policy and electoral support

The role of parties as providers of political education implies that electors vote for a party following a dispassionate examination of the policies which are put forward during an election contest and a calculated assessment as to which set of policies they deem to be the most preferable. But this is rarely the case. Most of us support a political party for reasons other than the policies which it puts forward. Factors such as our traditional loyalty to a party or its association with social class are likely to be more important than party policy when we decide how to vote.

Failure to provide political education

Parties may not seek to educate the public in any meaningful manner. Election campaigns may be conducted around trivia rather than key issues. Parties may be more concerned to denigrate an opponent than with an attempt to convince electors of the virtues of their own policies. Or they may decide that the wisest course of political action is to follow public opinion rather than seek to lead it. Thus ideology or policy which is viewed as unpopular might be abandoned by a party in an attempt to win elections.

Absence of popular involvement

We may also question the extent to which parties do genuinely permit widespread involvement in political affairs. French and Irish political parties, for example, lack a tradition of mass membership and tend to be controlled by small elitist groups. Nor are those who do join a party guaranteed a meaningful role in its affairs. The Italian Christian Democrats, for example, has a mass membership but this has little say on issues such as party policy. The formal accountability of party leaders to rank and file activists through mechanisms such as annual party conferences is often imperfectly achieved in practice due to the domination which leaders often exert over their parties.

Divisiveness

Political parties do not always seek to promote harmony. Some may seek to make political capital by accentuating existing divisions within society. The French *Front national* has sought to cultivate support by blaming that country's economic and social problems on immigration, especially from North Africa. The persecution of racial or religious groups, depicting them as the main cause of a country's problems, is a common tactic of the extreme Right and which serves to create social tension rather than harmony.

Self-Interest

Finally the role of parties as dispensers of patronage may result in accusations of 'jobs for the boys' or 'snouts in the trough'. This may result in popular disenchantment with the conduct of political affairs with politics being associated with the furtherance of self-interest or that of a ruling party's supporters.

Determinants of party systems

What factors influence the way in which political parties and party systems are formed, function and develop?

Considerable differences exist within liberal democracies concerning the nature of party systems. Some countries such as Britain, America and New Zealand have relatively few political parties. Scandinavia, however, is characterised by multiparty systems. In order to explain these differences we need to consider what factors influence the development of political parties.

The basis of party

The degree of homogeneity in a country is an important determinant concerning the formation and development of political parties. Basic cleavages within a society might provide the basis of party, reflecting its key divisions. These might include social class, nationalism, religion or race. Any of these factors are capable of providing the basis around which parties are established and subsequently operate. Some form of partisanship in which groups of electors have a strong affinity to a particular political party is crucial to sustain a stable party system.

Let us consider some examples of this:

Social class
In Britain social class was a key factor which shaped the development of political parties in the nineteenth and early years of the twentieth century. The landed aristocracy was identified with the Conservative party, the industrial bourgeoisie with the Liberal party and the working class with the Labour Party.

Religion
In France, Italy and Germany religion played an important part in providing the underpinning for political parties. In nineteenth century France the basic division was between clericals and anti-clericals. Today the vote for left wing parties is weakest where the influence of the Catholic Church is strongest, although by the 1960s social class began to play an increasingly important role in determining party affiliation. In Italy the Christian Democrats initially relied heavily on the Catholic vote while in Germany the coalition between the Christian Democrats and the Christian-Social Union represented a religious alliance between Catholics and Protestants in opposition to the Social Democrats who were viewed as representative of the secular interests within society.

Regionalism and nationalism
These factors may also provide the basis of party. Such may arise from a perception that the national government pays insufficient regard to the interests of people living in peripheral areas and is often underpinned by cultural factors. Regional or national autonomy is frequently demanded by such parties. Examples include the Italian *Lega Nord*, the Scottish National party, *Plaid Cymru* in Wales, the *Parti Québecois* in Quebec, Canada and the Catalan Republican Left and Basque National parties in Spain.

It follows from the above discussion that fundamental changes to a country's economic or social structure might have a significant effect on its political parties. The decline in jobs in the French steel, coal and shipbuilding industries has been cited as one explanation for the reduced support for the Communist Party. Immigration may influence the growth of racist political parties.

THE IRISH PARTY SYSTEM

Political parties may emerge when key social divisions are absent. This is the case in Ireland. Here a party system developed in the early twentieth century in a country which was relatively unified in terms of race, religion, language and social class. The key issue which divided the country was a matter of policy – support or opposition for the 1921 Anglo-Irish Treaty which accepted the partitioning of Ireland whereby six Irish counties remained part of the United Kingdom.

In response to this situation, two parties emerged – *Fine Gael* (which supported the treaty) and *Fianna Fáil* (which opposed it). However, as the treaty issue became irrelevant to the conduct of Irish politics, the parties remained as permanent entities. In this sense it might be argued that the parties became the cause of divisions in Ireland rather than reflections of them.

Political parties and electoral systems

It is sometimes argued that the electoral system has a major influence on the formation or operation of political parties. The first-past-the-post system is said to encourage the development of a relatively small number of parties since third parties are discriminated against. However, proportional representation facilitates the representation of minor parties in legislative bodies and thus, it is argued, promotes a multiparty system.

But we must be wary of unquestioning acceptance of the argument that proportional representation results in the development of a multiparty system. It might alternatively be argued that parties are based on factors such as social divisions within society rather than an electoral system. Thus proportional representation may be required to ensure that existing social divisions are represented in the composition of a country's legislature.

However, an electoral system may have some influence over the party system. The first-past-the-post system may encourage groups to align with a dominant political party in order to achieve their objectives. The British Conservative and Labour parties and the American Republican and Democratic parties illustrate this process. Groups are further encouraged to stay attached to a major party rather than split off and form smaller parties. These might become consigned to political oblivion due to the way in which this electoral system often works against the interests of minor parties.

THE FRENCH PARTY SYSTEM

In France the behaviour of political parties is influenced by the electoral system.

The second ballot system involves a number of second-round contests. Electors may be required to cast votes for candidates who do not represent the party of their choice. This, coupled with the emergence of the directly elected Presidency as the key political prize and the traditional core distinctions between Left and Right, encouraged major parties and/or their supporters to co-operate. This was referred to as bipolarisation.

Bipolarisation emerged during the 1970s and involved the major parties of the right and those of the left co-operating to contest elections. A two-bloc, four-party system emerged. In the case of the parties of the Left, electoral co-operation took shape as the formation of the Union of the Left which in 1974 narrowly failed to secure the election of François Mitterrand to the Presidency. Although subsequent changes to the structure of the French party system has affected this development, in both 1986 and 1993 the main parties on the Right presented a common programme for government.

The decline of party?

What changes have influenced the degree of support enjoyed by political parties recently?

In recent years the workings of political parties have been subject to scrutiny. Here we analyse the extent to which existing major parties have experienced losses in the level of support which they have traditionally enjoyed.

In Britain, 97% of the vote cast in the 1955 general election went to the Labour and Conservative parties. In 1964 this figure had declined to 88%. In 1992 it was further reduced to 76%. In France a similar picture occurred. In the 1981 legislative elections the four main parties (RPR, UDF, PCF and PS) secured 93% of the votes cast in the first round of elections. Subsequently there has been a significant move away from the two-bloc, four-party system. In 1993 the four main parties obtained 68% of the vote cast. Further, 2 million voters spoiled their ballots in the second round of the 1993 legislative elections rather than give their support to a major party candidate.

In the 1993 legislative elections the support for the Italian Christian Democrats dropped to below 30%. The decline in support for Germany's Social Democrats prompted this party to change its leader in 1995 while in Austria the traditional strength of the Christian Democrats and Social Democrats has been impaired by the increased support for the far Right Freedom party although the Social Democrats fared unexpectedly well in the 1995 emergency elections. In the United States the dominance of the two major parties was broken in the 1992 presidential election in which an independent candidate, Ross Perot, secured 19% of the total national vote.

Partisan dealignment

The loss of support for major parties is indicative of partisan dealignment. This term denotes that a large number of electors no longer see themselves as committed supporters who remain loyal to one particular political party. They may desert their traditional party for a minor party or become more discerning or inconsistent in their loyalty. One explanation which is often offered for partisan dealignment is class dealignment. This denotes that the historic attachment between social class and political party has become less pronounced. Factors such as the reduced intensity of the class conflict might account for such a phenomenon.

Class dealignment might be the prelude to realignment in which groups become the components of new coalitions which constitute the basis of party support. The formation of new coalitions is usually ratified in a realigning election and confirmed in subsequent ones. The American 1932 presidential election is an example of this which witnessed the birth of the 'New Deal coalition'. There is currently some debate in America as to whether President Reagan's victories in 1980 and 1984 were based on the emergence of a new coalition. The new preference of white males in the Southern states for the Republican Party seemed to denote a major shift in group loyalty from one major party to another. But such changes have not been sufficient to inaugurate an era of Republican dominance of the Presidency and Congress which was a feature of the strength of the New Deal coalition for the Democratic Party after 1932.

The notion of class dealignment is not unchallenged as an explanation for the loss of support by parties which depended on this source of electoral backing. For example, the reduced level of support for the British Labour party after 1979 might be attributed to the smaller size of the working class rather than any significant drop in the level of its support for that party.

The continued vitality of political parties

In the light of what has been discussed above, is the position of the established political parties in jeopardy?

It might seem that established political parties face the prospects of losing support and of being unable to discharge the functions with which they have traditionally been associated. However, it seems likely that they will continue to carry out important roles within liberal democratic political systems. This is because parties are adaptable and understand the importance of reform.

Reforms to restore the vitality of parties may take a number of different forms. It includes attempts to increase the number of citizens joining such organisations. In countries such as America, where local parties have often been controlled by 'bosses', initiatives to increase party membership have sometimes been accompanied by reforms designed to 'democratise' the workings of political parties and ensure that members are able to exercise a greater degree of control over key party affairs including the selection of candidates and the formulation of policy.

There have been problems associated with such developments. Increasing the membership of local parties has sometimes (although not consistently) resulted in accusations of extremists 'taking over' control of organisations which in turn makes it difficult for parties to appeal to a wide electoral base in order to win elections. What is termed 'coalition building' in America becomes difficult if a party is associated with extremist issues. Similar problems beset the British Labour Party in the early 1980s which resulted in that party's disastrous showing in the 1983 general election in which it abandoned social democracy and placed a manifesto before the electorate based on fundamentalist socialist principles. These policies emerged as a result of reforms designed to democratise that organisation by giving rank-and-file members a greater role in party affairs, principally the selection of party candidates and the party leader.

In this concluding section we examine in greater detail the initiatives which have been developed by American political parties to address the issue of decline.

The reform of American political parties

The decay of party has been especially pronounced in America. In Britain a candidate's party label is crucial is securing support. In America elections have tended to be candidate-centred. Incumbent office-holders use their record as a source of electoral support and candidates utilise personal organisation and fund-raising. Such factors have served to weaken the role performed by parties in political affairs. However, attempts have been made to rectify this situation. The workings of political parties in the United States have been subject to a number of reforming initiatives directed at the process of nominating candidates and the role of parties in election campaigns.

Reform to the nominating process was particularly associated with the Democratic party and arose following the 1968 national convention. The McGovern-Fraser Commission, 1969, (and the subsequent reform commissions of Mikulski and Winigrad in the 1970s) succeeded in initiating a number of developments. These included broadening the nomination process at the expense of the control formerly exercised by party leaders, increasing the size and demographic representativeness of the National Convention and the National Committee and introducing a charter containing rules and procedures governing key party activities, thus enhancing the control exercised by the central party organs over local parties.

Such developments tended to democratise the workings of the Democratic Party, although subsequent measures undertaken in the 1980s (especially the enhanced status given to selected party members, the 'superdelegates') did not proceed in this direction. The Republican Party was less influenced by this process although state and local parties did sometimes adopt a compatible course of action.

The Republican Party initially attempted to revitalise the role played by parties in election campaigns. This objective was especially associated with Bill Brock who chaired the Republican National Committee between 1977 and 1981. It resulted in this body performing a more constant and active role in electioneering. This course of action was also adopted by the Democrats. Its adoption was influenced by the fortunes of these parties (the poor showing of the Republicans in the 1974 and 1976 elections and the Democrats' loss of the presidency and their weak congressional performance in 1980).

The importance of parties at election times has been enhanced but there are limits to what has been achieved. In particular the 1974 Federal Election Campaign Act and its subsequent amendments ensured that parties would not dominate the election process as they do in other liberal democracies by placing curbs on party fund-raising activities. However, the role of parties has become more prominent in regard to the money they raise and the services which they are able to provide. The ability of the national party organs to give or withhold aid at election times has tended to enhance their power at the expense of state and local parties.

Questions

1 What reasons would you put forward to support the argument that political parties are indispensable to the workings of liberal democratic systems of government?
2 What factors limit the extent to which popular involvement in political affairs is facilitated by political parties?
3 With reference to any country with which you are familiar, draw up a list of main points which differentiate the main political parties in respect of the electoral support which they obtain and the ideology and policies which they put forward.
4 Analyse the evidence which suggests that major political parties are 'in decline'. Why has this development occurred, and what might such parties do in order to reverse this trend?

Summary

1 A political party is an organisation with a formal structure whose main role is to contest elections in the hope of securing political power.
2 Parties are guided by ideology which provides a fundamental statement of the values on which its policies are based.
3 Parties perform a number of important roles in liberal democratic political systems. These include.
   - recruiting and selecting candidates for public office: in particular national leaders emerge through party organisation;
   - providing governments with organised support;
   - facilitating popular interest and participation in political affairs;
   - promoting national harmony through the 'aggregation of interests';
   - acting as a source of patronage.
4 However, parties do not always fulfil the above roles effectively. They do not all possess mass membership or seek to permit widespread involvement in policy formulation. Some heighten, rather than heal, existing social divisions.
5 The basis of party is provided by factors such as class, race or religion. The electoral system may have a bearing on the workings of the party system.
6 In recent years it has been argued that parties are in decline. This may be evidenced by the loss of support experienced by established political parties. These have suffered from partisan dealignment which may be due to class dealignment. This situation may provide the basis for realignment.
7 Parties have tackled the problems which they face by initiating various reforms which are designed to sustain the roles they perform within liberal democratic political structures.

5

PRESSURE GROUPS

Definition

What is a pressure group?

A pressure group is an organisation with a formal structure which is composed of a number of individuals seeking to further a common cause or interest. These groups operate at all levels of society. Some seek to influence the activities of local or central government. Others exist within the workplace in the form of trade unions. The factions or tendencies found within some political parties are further examples of such organisations. Many groups perform functions which are not political, for example by providing benefits or advisory services either to their members or to the general public. For the purposes of our discussion, however, we shall concentrate on those seeking to exert influence over national government policy making.

PRESSURE GROUPS AND SOCIAL MOVEMENTS

Many reforms are promoted by organisations termed 'social movements'. Examples include the Peace Movement, the Women's Movement and the Environmental Movement. But it is not easy to differentiate precisely between these and pressure groups.

Social movements tend to be loosely organised in comparison to pressure groups and their focus of concern is often broader. Rather than concentrate on one specific policy area, their con-

---

cern is to instil new moral values within society. They may, however, embrace the activities of pressure groups whose specific aims are compatible with this overall objective. We would, for example, place the British Campaign for Nuclear Disarmament within the umbrella of the Peace Movement.

Social movements typically operate outside of mainstream political institutions and their tactics are thus dominated by non-conventional forms of political activity. This is frequently carried out on an international stage rather than being confined to any particular country.

The role of pressure groups

What activities are performed by pressure groups?

Pressure groups seek to influence policy makers. Their actions are thus directed at politicians, civil servants and, in some cases, the general public. The complex and lengthy nature of the policy-making process provides wide scope for group activity.

A major concern of pressure groups is to persuade policy makers to consider their views and then to act upon them. This involves inducing policy makers either to adopt a course of action which they did not initially intend to embark upon or to abandon a measure which they had originally decided to introduce. If a group succeeds in getting its views acted upon it may also become involved in further stages of the policy-making process. These include participating in the formulation of policy to achieve the objective(s) which the group successfully placed on the political agenda. Pressure groups may also be concerned with the implementation of that policy and with monitoring it to ensure that the desired aims are achieved.

PRESSURE GROUPS AND NON-GOVERNMENTAL BODIES

Our discussion of pressure groups is primarily concerned with their influence on central government policy making. However, pressure groups frequently direct their activities towards alternative targets. Such may include the practices adopted by commercial organisations. Indeed, a number of Greenpeace activists see business rather than politics as the best arena within which to further environmental aims.

One example of this was the activity mounted by the environmental organisation Greenpeace in 1995 against the decision by the Shell Oil company to sink a disused oil rig, Brent Spar, in the North Atlantic. Adverse publicity coupled with boycotts against Shell's products organised by environmental groups resulted in the company agreeing to examine alternative ways of disposing of the redundant rig.

Political parties and pressure groups

What is the difference between a political party and a pressure group?

The key words for us to consider are 'control' and 'influence'.

Political parties normally seek control over the policy-making process. They may achieve this through their own efforts or in combination with other political parties. They contest elections in the hope of securing power so that they can carry out the policies contained in their election manifestos. Such policies cover all aspects of public affairs and the party seeks to exercise control over a wide range of issues. Pressure groups wish to influence those who control the policy-making process. They do not normally have an interest in the overall work of government but only in those aspects of its operations which are of concern to the group and its membership. In order to pursue their aims, groups usually possess a degree of autonomy from both government and political parties. Thus while a pressure group seeks to exert influence over a relatively narrow aspect of policy making, a political party wishes to control the overall direction of public affairs.

One further distinction between political parties and pressure groups concerns the manner in which they seek to cultivate support. Political parties concentrate their activities on the general public, hoping to convince voters to support them in election contests. Although campaigns directed at the public may form one aspect of pressure group campaigning, the tactics at their disposal are more diverse. Influence may be sought at all levels of the political system.

Classification of pressure groups

How can we distinguish between the wide range of pressure groups which operate within liberal democracies?

Various ways may be adopted to classify the pressure groups which are to be found within liberal democratic political systems. One method is to differentiate according to the relationship which exists between the objective put forward by the group and its membership. This provides us with two broad categories into which groups might be placed.

Sectional groups

These are groups in which the members have a vested interest in the success of their organisation. They stand to benefit materially if the aims of the group are adopted by policy makers. Such organisations are sometimes referred to as 'interest' or 'economic' groups. The membership of sectional groups tends to be narrow and restrictive, drawn from people with similar backgrounds. In Britain examples include employers' associations (such as the Confederation of British Industry), professional bodies (such as the British Medical Association) or labour organisations (such as the Transport and General Workers' Union). American examples include the American Bar Association and the American Medical Association.

Promotional (or cause) groups

These are organisations in which the members are united in support of a cause which does not necessarily benefit them directly. They tend to view the work of the group as a moral concern and their aim is to change social attitudes and values. Examples include the American organisation, Common Cause, which seeks honesty and efficiency in government. The aims of promotional groups may be designed to benefit specific groups (especially minorities whose needs are often ignored by policy makers) or be directed at an issue affecting society as a whole. Membership of a promotional group is open to all who share its objectives: members are typically drawn from a wide range of social or occupational backgrounds and are united solely by their common support for the cause advocated by the organisation.

BODIES OTHER THAN PRESSURE GROUPS MAY SEEK INFLUENCE

Pressure group activity is not confined to organisations which are specifically established to advance an interest or a cause. It may also be performed by bodies whose existence is concerned with other functions but which may, on occasions, act in the capacity of a pressure group and seek to exert influence within the policy-making process.

The Catholic Church in Ireland is an example of a body which sometimes acts as a pressure group. The Roman Catholic bishops played a prominent role in the 1995 referendum campaign opposing a change in the Irish constitution to permit divorce.

In Britain chief constables and senior members of the judiciary have sometimes made public pronouncements designed to influence the approach adopted by policy makers to the operations of the criminal justice system and in America the Pentagon sometimes performs a role akin to that of a pressure group on behalf of the military establishment.

The activities of pressure groups

How do pressure groups seek to exert influence on policy makers?

Pressure groups operate throughout the governmental system. In this section we examine the main areas which form the focus of group activity.

The executive branch of government

This consists of both ministers and civil servants. Some pressure groups are able to maintain constant liaison with, and be consulted by, these key policy makers.

The relationship between groups and the executive branch of government may be constructed in a number of ways. Some have a permanent relationship with government departments. Members representing a group may be appointed to joint advisory committees which are mechanisms through which the concerns of a pressure group can be made known to the relevant government department.

Alternatively some pressure groups enjoy regular access to civil servants and they may also be involved in discussions on appointments to bodies which are responsible to a department. In some countries contact is secured through the 'old boy' network, in which former ministers or civil servants secure jobs in organisations which may benefit from the contacts in government possessed by such former public officials.

Groups in this position are termed 'insider' groups. This denotes the close relationship which some groups enjoy with key members of the policy-making process. It is a desirable position to occupy in a country such as Britain where political power is centralised in the executive branch of government although it is equally important in some federal countries such as Australia. The relationship between the British National Farmers' Union and the Ministry of Agriculture, Fisheries and Food is an example of such an 'insider' relationship.

Other groups may secure influence from their relationship with the government in power. This was the case in Britain between 1964 and 1970 when leading trade unionists were frequently invited to Downing Street to discuss industrial affairs over 'beer and sandwiches'. This politically-fashioned link with the ministerial component of the executive is not permanent and may alter when the government changes. This happened in Britain after 1979 when the Conservative administration adopted a more hostile attitude to the trade unions than had been the case when Labour governments were in power.

PRESSURE GROUPS AND GOVERNMENT

The ideology of political parties and the policies which they pursue in government is one factor which influences pressure group effectiveness.

The introduction of monetarist economic policies in Britain after 1979 and in New Zealand after 1984 had an adverse effect on the role which organised interests such as trade unions were able to exert over public policy making.

The legislature

There are a number of ways whereby pressure groups may seek to exert influence over the legislature. A major mechanism is that of lobbying.

Lobbying was originally directed exclusively at legislators. Its aim is to ensure that these law makers are fully briefed and are thus in a position to advance the interests of the pressure group when issues which are relevant to it come before the legislature for discussion or resolution. The importance attached to this activity is much influenced by the independence of action which legislatures possess. Pressure groups may devote relatively little attention to such bodies if they perceive them to be dominated by the executive branch of government.

In America many groups employ professional lobbyists. These are full-time officials who work in Washington and constantly subject members of both houses of Congress to the views and attitudes of the organisations which employ them. Although such activities also occur in Britain, the strength of the party system may serve to reduce the effectiveness of pressure group activity directed at this branch of government.

Pressure groups may voice their concerns to the legislature through ways other than lobbying. In the Fourth French Republic some groups such as the trade unions and farmers' associations enjoyed permanent membership of specialised legislative standing committees. In both Britain and America investigations conducted by the legislature provide a mechanism for the articulation of group interests, while in Germany the committee system utilised by the *Bundestag* serves to enhance pressure group influence over legislation.

IRON TRIANGLES

In America some pressure groups enjoy considerable power from the relationship which they have constructed with both the executive and legislative branches of government.

The term 'iron triangle' has been used to describe the close links (governed by ties of interdependent self-interest) which exist between an interest group, the government department or agency concerned with the interests espoused by that organisation and the Congressional committee charged with responsibility for that policy area. Each element of the 'triangle' provides services, information or policy for the others.

Although this arrangement provides some groups with a powerful position from which its interests can be advanced, it has
been argued that it is responsible for decentralising and fragmenting the policy-making process to the detriment of the
exercise of central control by the executive and legislative
branches of government. In more recent years, the autonomy
of such 'sub-governments' has been challenged by alternative
centres of power (such as issue networks).

The judiciary

Pressure groups may utilise the courts in their attempts to secure the
adoption of their aims, usually by challenging the legality of legislation. This approach was crucial to the American civil rights movement. Organisations such as the National Association for the
Advancement of Colored People used this mechanism in their fight
against segregation practised by a number of the Southern States. A
landmark in education was reached in 1954 when the Supreme Court
ruled (in the case of *Brown* v. *Board of Education of Topeka*) that segregation in schools was unconstitutional and thus illegal throughout
the entire country.

In more recent years American consumer, producer and environmental
groups have turned to the courts to advance their concerns. President
Clinton's attempt in 1995 to introduce measures to reduce teenage
smoking was immediately countered by law suits filed by five cigarette
manufacturing companies, asking the courts to block such initiatives.

Rules governing the operations of a country's judicial system have a
major bearing on the ability or willingness of pressure groups to use
the courts to further their objectives. In Australia, for example, it is
difficult for pressure groups to initiate legal actions since it is
necessary for plaintiffs to demonstrate a personal stake or material
interest in a case. In America, however, interests groups are permitted
to present arguments directly to courts.

The role of the courts is less prominent in countries such as Britain
and New Zealand where judicial challenge to national legislation is
precluded by the concept of parliamentary sovereignty, but pressure
groups may utilise the courts and launch test cases (when the law is

in need of clarification) or challenge the legality of the way in which the law has been implemented.

Political parties

Pressure groups may forge close links with political parties and use them to further their aims. Parties may incorporate aspects of a group's demands within their own policy statements. The American AFL-CIO is associated with the Democratic Party while the French CGT has close ties with the Communist Party. The relationship which exists between pressure groups and political parties may be organisational or financial. In Britain leading trade unions are affiliated to the Labour Party while the Conservatives receive funding and support from the business sector.

Public opinion

Most pressure groups do not enjoy the status of 'insiders' and are kept at arm's length by politicians and civil servants. The latter often adopt a hostile attitude towards groups as they may provide politicians with information which rivals that presented to a minister by a government department. This may have an adverse effect on the role performed by civil servants in the policy-making process. Accordingly pressure groups may seek to secure influence by mobilising public opinion behind the policies advocated by the group. Policy makers thus become subject to the influence exerted by orchestrated public opinion.

There are a number of ways which may be used by pressure groups to secure public endorsement of their aims. A basic division exists, however, behind tactics which are designed to educate the public into positively and enthusiastically supporting the objectives of a group and those which seek to apply a form of sanction to coerce the public into applying pressure on policy makers to accede to the group's demands. The intention of the coercive approach is to make the public inconvenienced, anxious or even frightened so that they exert pressure on the policy makers to give into the demands of the group. The strike weapon used by trade unionists sometimes provides an example of the coercive approach especially when such a sanction seeks to alter government economic or industrial policy. Indiscriminate terrorism, randomly directed against the public, is an extreme example of an attempt to alter the direction of government policy by coercive means.

PRESSURE GROUPS AND THE PUBLIC

Pressure groups often take their case 'to the streets' and seek to mobilise public support for their objectives. In doing this they seek to influence policy makers by demonstrating the extent of public support for their views.

In Britain, for example, protests organised by animal welfare groups such as Compassion in World Farming occurred at ports and airports during 1995. These were directed against the export of British calves for the Continental veal trade.

Direct action

Pressure groups may go beyond seeking support for their cause and engage in various forms of direct action to further it. This may involve breaking the law in the hope that the dignity of the objective will create public sympathy for the group's aims. Public support may be secured through activities which publicise issues (such as the plight of the homeless or the treatment of animals in research laboratories) which were hitherto generally unknown or when those engaged in such activities are responded to in a manner which public opinion deems to be unwarranted or unacceptable. The destruction of the ship *Rainbow Warrior* by French divers in Auckland harbour in 1985, resulting in the death of a photographer, was widely viewed as an unreasonable response to environmental protesters.

DIRECT ACTION

Pressure groups may seek to achieve their objectives by undertaking activities which physically implement them.

The occupation of empty property by squatters' groups is one example of this. In early 1995 a campaign of occupation in Paris led by the Catholic priest, Abbé Pierre, resulted in the then mayor, Jacques Chirac, agreeing to requisition a number of empty office buildings to provide the homeless with shelter for the winter.

A further example of direct action is associated with American and French pro-life groups who seek to secure further their opposition to abortion by blockading the clinics where such operations are performed.

Protest directed at the government

The mobilisation of public opinion constitutes an indirect form of pressure which a group may employ to secure influence over policy. Public opinion is an intermediary between the group and the policy makers. However, groups may seek to secure influence over policy by deploying the tactics of protest directly at the policy makers. This is a relatively common occurrence in France where institutionalised links between groups and policy makers are not strongly developed. Such tactics are frequently utilised by groups seeking to alter the direction of government policy. A recent example of this is the wave of industrial disputes and public demonstrations which occurred towards the end of 1995 directed at the austerity programme of the French prime minister, Alain Juppé, which sought to cut welfare benefits.

The international arena

Pressure groups do not confine their activities to one country but increasingly operate on a world stage. They may be international organisations seeking the universal adoption of standards of behaviour throughout the world. Groups such as Amnesty International (which is concerned with human rights) is an example of such a body. Alternatively groups may be formed in one country seeking influence over policy making in another. The Greek Animal Welfare Fund, for example, is a London-based organisation which seeks to alter the official and public attitudes towards the treatment accorded to animals in Greece.

Pressure groups have also adapted to the development of supranational governmental organisations. The policy makers of the European Union (principally the Commission and Council of Ministers) are subject to pressure group activity. Organisations within individual countries may co-ordinate their activities with similar groups in other countries in order to secure overall influence on European Union policy. An umbrella body for farming interests (COPA) and an employers' federation (UNICE) reflect the European-wide dimension to these groups' activities. Pressure groups may also establish permanent machinery to further their interests within supranational bodies such as the European Union. An example of this is the Brussels Office of the Confederation of British Industry which monitors developments in the European Union and seeks to influence the direction of European legislation to the benefit of its membership.

International institutions such as the United Nations Human Rights Committee and the European Court of Justice have also been used by pressure groups who seek to question the actions undertaken by individual governments. In Britain, for example, groups opposed to motorway construction have exercised their right to complain to the European Commission that the government failed to adequately implement the procedures of the 1988 Directive concerned with Environmental Impact Assessments. If the Commission decided that there was a case to answer the government can be taken to the European Court of Justice for contravening European law.

Pressure group influence

What factors determine whether a pressure group is likely to be successful in furthering its aims?

The ability of a group to mobilise support

The level of support enjoyed by a group may be one determinant of its strength. Successful groups need to represent all who adhere to a particular interest or a specific cause. The fragmentation of French labour organisations into a number of competing federations has tended to weaken their influence over policy makers and is in contrast to the organisational unity of business interests (whose trade associations are linked by the umbrella organisation, CNPF). The strength of American labour organisations is reduced by the low affiliation rate of workers to trade unions. The cause of animal welfare in Britain may be impeded by the proliferation of organisations which include the Royal Society for the Prevention of Cruelty to Animals, Compassion in World Farming, the Animal Liberation Front and the International Fund For Animal Welfare.

PRESSURE GROUP STRENGTH

One development designed to enhance group strength is the banding together of bodies with similar objectives under the auspices of an umbrella organisation. Examples of such 'associations of associations' include Britain's Trades Union Congress and Confederation of British Industry and Australia's National Farmers' Federation.

Expertise commanded by a group

A further factor which may affect the influence groups exercise over policy making is the expertise which they are able to command. Governments may be reliant upon such bodies for advice on the technical and complex issues which surround much contemporary public policy and may further be reliant on a group's goodwill or support to implement policy. Such considerations had a major bearing on the influence possessed by the British Medical Association following the establishment of the National Health Service in 1946.

Resources possessed by a group

The resources which pressure groups are able to command may also determine the success or failure of a group. New technology (such as computer-processed direct mail) is expensive. Economically powerful groups possess the ability to publicise their objectives and also to resist sanctions which may be deployed against them. Employer organisations are often influential for such reasons. By contrast, consumer groups have traditionally suffered from lack of resources which may help to explain their difficulties in securing influence over the actions of policy makers. However some governments (such as the French) and supranational bodies (such as the European Union) have contributed towards the funding of pressure groups which offsets those weaknesses which derive from lack of funds.

Sanctions available to a group

Finally, the sanctions which an organisation is able to deploy may be a factor in its ability to influence policy making. Investment decisions or strikes may be used as weapons by business groups or trade unions to influence the conduct of policy makers. Groups involved in the implementation of public policy possess the ability to withhold their co-operation and thus prevent the progress of policies to which they object.

The strengths and weaknesses of pressure group activity

The role performed by pressure groups is said to be beneficial to the operations of liberal democratic political systems. Why, therefore, are their activities sometimes criticised?

To answer this question we need to examine the benefits which pressure groups bring to liberal democratic political systems and then to assess the disadvantages which may arise.

Benefits of pressure groups

The main benefits associated with the activities of pressure groups are as follows:

Popular involvement in policy making
Pressure groups ensure that the policy making process is not monopolised by politicians or senior civil servants. The control which they are able to exercise is to some extent offset by the operations of such groups, whose involvement may be institutionalised. In France, for example, advisory councils composed of representatives of interest groups, technicians and prominent personalities appointed by the government are attached to individual ministries. Additionally these organisations facilitate the participation of members of the general public in policy making whose role in political affairs is thus not merely confined to casting a vote in periodic elections.

Political education
The need for pressure groups to 'sell' their case in order to secure influence may aid the process of public education in political affairs. Groups may need to explain what they believe in and why they endorse the views which they hold. Groups who oppose government policy may engage in activities such as investigative journalism which results in enhanced scrutiny and popular awareness of government activity.

Promote reform
Pressure groups may also raise matters which the major political parties would prefer to ignore either because they do not consider them to be mainstream political issues which generally dominate election campaigns (such as the economy or law and order) or because they are internally divisive. The emergence of women's issues and environmental concerns onto the political agenda owed much to the activities of pressure groups.

However, pressure groups do not always perform such a progressive role. The stance taken by the National Rifle Association in America towards President Clinton's Crime Bill in 1994 demonstrated the negative role which groups sometimes perform in resisting reform proposals which they view as contrary to the interests of their members.

Articulate minority interests

The workings of liberal democratic political systems may also benefit from the ability of pressure groups to articulate minority opinions or concerns. Liberal democracies tend to pay most heed to majority opinion. There is thus a risk that minorities get ignored. Pressure groups provide a vehicle whereby minorities can articulate their needs and encourage policy makers to pay heed to them. In the 1960s the British group Campaign Against Racial Discrimination sought to voice the opinions of ethnic minority communities. This group's activities was one factor which led to the passage of the 1965 Race Relations Act.

Disadvantages of pressure groups

Inequality

One problem associated with pressure groups is that all are not accorded the same degree of attention by policy makers. The influence they are able to command is considerably influenced by factors which include the resources at the group's disposal and the relationships they have constructed with government departments. There are two diametrically opposed problems which arise from the inequality which exists between groups.

First, this situation may result in worthy minority causes making little impact on public policy as they are relatively ignored by bureaucrats, ministers, political parties, the media and public opinion. Members of groups in such a position may become frustrated and resort to violence, seeking to coerce when they are denied opportunities to persuade.

Alternatively factors such as resources and sanctions may result in some groups occupying a powerful position within the policy-making process. The ability of some groups to command considerable economic resources and be in possession of powerful sanctions which it can deploy to further its interests may result in them being in a position not merely to influence but to dominate the policy-making process. The power of large American corporations has for long provided them with a wide degree of autonomy in their dealings with government. In its most extreme form confrontation may result between the group and the government when the issue is, effectively, one of 'who governs'?

Internal democracy

A further difficulty which we encounter with the workings of pressure groups is the extent to which the opinions or actions of the leadership faithfully reflect the views of the membership. The belief by British Conservative governments that trade unions, for example, sometimes endorsed political activity which was not genuinely supported by the rank and file resulted in a number of pieces of legislation being enacted during the 1980s designed to ensure that such organisations were responsive to their members' opinions. These measures included requirements for compulsory secret ballots to be held before the commencement of strike action and the periodic election of union leaders. However, most pressure groups are not subject to such internal regulation and are thus susceptible to domination by their leaders. In this situation pressure groups fail to greatly extend the degree of popular involvement in policy making.

Methods used to secure influence

Concern has been expressed within liberal democracies regarding the expenditure of money by pressure groups in order to achieve influence. The purposes of such spending may go beyond political education and extend into activities which are perceived to approximate bribery or corruption. Lobbying has been a particular cause of concern and has led some countries to introduce measures to regulate such activities. In America, for example, the 1946 Federal Regulation of Lobbying Act required lobbyists both to register and state their policy goals. Registration for Canadian lobbyists was introduced by the 1988 Lobbyists Registration Act.

POLITICAL ACTION COMMITTEES

In America Political Action Committees (PACs) were established in 1974 as a mechanism through which groups can direct funds into the individual campaign funds of candidates who supported their aims. PACs are set up by pressure groups and registered with the Federal Election Commission. This procedure permits groups to collect money from their members which is then donated – via the PAC – to political campaigns. The number of such bodies has risen dramatically – from about 800 in 1974 to almost 4,000 ten years later.

The support which can be given to individual candidates has

---

been limited by subsequent amendments to the 1974 legislation, but PACs are able to initiate independent political action. One form this may take is to campaign against the election of candidates to whom they are opposed. PACs have also been accused of weakening the role of local party organisation by reducing the importance of its fund-raising activities and thereby reducing the level of public participation in election campaigns.

The corporate state

A final problem which is associated with pressure groups arises when a relatively small number enjoy a close relationship with the executive branch of government. The content of public policy may be heavily influenced by leaders of key pressure groups (especially employer and labour organisations) if they are accorded privileged access to ministers and civil servants through institutional arrangements which effectively incorporate these groups into the state's decision-making machinery. The term 'corporate state' is applied to such political arrangements.

Policy makers frequently consult with pressure groups in liberal democracies. Bodies which include Britain's National Economic Development Council facilitate such discussions. In France the Constitution requires the government to consult with the Economic and Social Council on socio-economic legislation. This body contains civil servants, trade unions, farmers' organisations, business associations and professional groups. The nature of the political system changes, however, if these consultations preclude the involvement of other parties and lead to consensual decisions being taken which cannot be meaningfully discussed in other forums. Elections cease to enable the public to exert influence over the content of policy while legislatures may be relegated to bodies which rubber-stamp decisions taken elsewhere but over which they possess little or no control. An additional concern is the lack of accountability of policy makers in such corporate structures. Meetings involving pressure groups, ministers and civil servants are conducted in secret, away from the public gaze. It is difficult to ascertain where precisely power resides and who can be held responsible for particular decisions.

PLURALISM AND HYPERPLURALISM

Power in a pluralist society is dispersed. Policy emerges as the result of competition, consultation, bargaining and conciliation conducted between groups who are accorded relatively equal access to the policy-making arena. This process is overseen by the government which is viewed as a neutral arbitrator. Pressure groups thus perform a crucial role in policy making.

A problem may arise, however, in a society in which a very wide range of groups emerge, some of which hold diametrically opposing views. The processes of consultation, bargaining and conciliation may be long and drawn out. The decision-making process may stagnate and governments find it difficult, or impossible, to take any decisions. This situation (which regards all interests being on an equal footing) is known as 'hyperpluralism'. However, the tendency for powerful groups (including the government) to dominate the policy-making process serves to reduce the likelihood of such stagnation occurring in many liberal democracies.

Questions

1 What is a pressure group and how does it differ from a political party?
2 List any six pressure groups with whose work you are familiar and identify the issues which they seek to further. Would you classify these groups as sectional or promotional bodies?
3 Place yourself in the position of a member of a pressure group whose objective is to convince central government to invest more money in railways at the expense of motorway construction. Consider the material discussed in the sections 'The activities of pressure groups' and 'Pressure group influence' in this chapter and then evaluate the strengths and weaknesses of methods which might be used to influence policy makers to endorse this objective.
4 You have been asked to make a short speech in a debate on pressure groups. Based on your reading of the section 'The strengths and weaknesses of pressure group activity' in this chapter, would you conclude that pressure groups are harmful or beneficial to the operations of liberal democratic political systems?

Summary

1 Pressure groups seek to secure influence over policy makers in those areas which are of concern to them. Unlike political parties they do not seek power or control over the entire operations of government.

2 A wide variety of pressure groups exist within liberal democracies. There is a key differentiation, however, between sectional and promotional groups. Sectional groups are those whose members stand to personally benefit from the successful operations of the group whereas promotional groups are primarily concerned with changing the moral values of society.

3 Pressure groups may employ a range of tactics in order to influence policy making. These include:
   - liaison with ministers and civil servants in the executive branch of government (through mechanisms such as advisory committees);
   - seeking to ensure that members of the legislature are aware of the group's policies – lobbying is one way to achieve this objective;
   - using the courts to advance group demands;
   - procuring influence over the policy adopted by major political parties;
   - taking the group's case 'to the streets' and using the weight of public opinion to exert influence on the policy makers;
   - engaging in direct action.

   Pressure groups are increasingly international in scope and seek to further their interests outside of their country of origin. Pressure groups have adapted their organisation and activities to influence supranational bodies such as the European Union.

4 Pressure groups are not equally influential. Their ability to influence public policy is determined by factors such as the extent to which a group represents all adherents to a cause or interest, the expertise and resources which a group is able to command and the sanctions which it may deploy to further its policies.

5 Pressure groups bring a number of advantages to the operations of liberal democratic political systems. These include reducing the power of politicians and civil servants, facilitating popular involvement in policy making, improving the public's knowledge of political affairs, raising issues which the mainstream parties ignore and advancing the concerns of minorities.

However, pressure groups have been subject to criticism. It has been argued that some get preferential treatment in their dealings with policy makers, that the views expressed by their leaders are not necessarily held by the membership and that activities such as lobbying are ineffectively regulated. The relationship occupied by certain key groups in a state's decision-making process may alter its fundamental political arrangements and result in the emergence of a corporate state.

6

THE MEDIA

The role of the media in a liberal democracy

What is understood by the term 'media' and why does such perform an important role within a liberal democracy?

The media is a mechanism of communication: historically it mainly consisted of newspapers but today the media is more diverse. It includes journals, radio, television and newer means of communication using computer technology. The Internet is an example of the latter. This consists of networks of computers linked by the international telephone system through which information can be disseminated.

THE INTERNET

The Internet is developing into a major mechanism of international communication and is becoming widely utilised in political affairs. For example, in 1995 details of the British Chancellor of the Exchequer's Budget were circulated by this means of communication.

There are, however, a number of problems associated with the Internet. These include the extent to which personal data becomes available to a wider audience than has a legitimate interest in such information, and the issue of regulation. At the end of 1995 an American company, CompuServe Inc, closed worldwide access to some 200 sex discussion forums available on the Internet following allegations that some of these

---

> were distributing child pornography. The Munich prosecutor initiated an action in connection with this.
>
> This raised two issues – the adequacy of the regulation of material circulated on the Internet and the extent to which national laws could, effectively, impose censorship on a worldwide basis.

We now consider the importance of the functions performed by the media in the operations of a liberal democratic political system.

A source of information

First, the media is a source of information concerning internal and international events. By reading, listening or viewing the media, members of the general public are informed about events of which they have no first-hand knowledge and thereby become more politically aware. One advantage of this is that public participation in policy making is facilitated. Public opinion is able to exert pressure on governments over a wide range of matters which, but for the role of the media, would be confined to the knowledge of a relatively small, elite group of rulers. The problems facing minorities can be made more widely known in this manner.

Scrutiny of government

The media acts as a watchdog and scrutinises the activities performed by governments. The electorate has information placed at its disposal with which it can judge the record of governments: in particular the shortcomings or errors committed by individual ministers or by the government as a whole may be exposed. Investigative journalism has especially aided this role, whose impact was spectacularly displayed in the downfall of President Nixon in 1974 in connection with the Watergate break-in. In this manner the media performs an important function by ensuring that governments can be held effectively accountable to the electorate.

'The fourth estate'

The term 'fourth estate' is often used to describe this role of the media as a guardian of a country's constitution and its liberal democratic system of politics. This implies, however, that the media possesses autonomy and is independent of the state, the institutions which comprise it (including the political parties) and the economic interests which underlay it.

Problems posed by the media

If, as has been argued, the media performs vital tasks in the effective functioning of a liberal democratic system of government, why are its operations frequently subject to criticism?

While it is generally accepted that the media is important to the functioning of liberal democracy, its operations are frequently subject to adverse comment. Below we consider the major criticisms which have been made concerning the manner in which the media operates.

Partisanship

The first problem is that of partisanship. Although in countries such as Britain and Ireland radio and television are subject to legislation which is designed to prevent programmes favouring one politician or political party at the expense of another, other sections of the media, especially the press, are politically biased: they may support one party which they portray in a favourable light while seeking to denigrate its political opponents.

Press bias is primarily effected through analysis: that is, newspapers do not simply report events, but seek to guide the public to a particular interpretation of those occurrences and the manner in which problems might be resolved. One way this is done is by blurring fact and opinion. This results in a story which is slanted towards a political perspective which the newspaper wishes to advance.

Partisanship is not necessarily a problem: if a country possesses a press which is diverse, a relatively wide range of political opinion will be presented. The biases of one newspaper, for example, can be offset by another presenting a totally different report or analysis of the same issue. Most members of the general public, however, do not read a wide range of newspapers to secure such a balanced view. We tend to be selective in our choice of newspaper and thus may be influenced by the interpretation which it puts forward.

Further, newspapers rarely reflect the wide range of political views and opinions found within a particular country. In Britain, for example, the bulk of national newspapers support the Conservative Party. In Germany they tend to articulate a moderate conservative political position. This problem of bias has been compounded by recent developments in the concentration of ownership. In many liberal democracies a number of newspapers are owned or controlled by one individual which may restrict the diversity of views expressed in that nation's press. Examples of such 'press barons' include Silvio Berlusconi in Italy, the Springer Group in Germany and Rupert Murdoch whose worldwide interests constitute a media empire on which, it has been said, the sun never sets.

Selective coverage of events

A second criticism which is sometimes levelled against the media concerns the process by which events are selected for coverage. It is argued that stories which appear in our newspapers or on our television screens are not chosen according to their importance but, rather, their presence is determined by the criterion of 'newsworthiness' applied by media owners or editors. This may mean that stories which are sensational get media coverage at the expense of worthier events which lack such 'glamour'. Thus war coverage or an inner city riot may get coverage at the expense of events such as famines simply because editors believe that the spectre of a tenement block being bombed or a police car being burned is more likely to attract readers or boost listening or viewing figures than is a story of quiet and resigned suffering which lacks such drama.

This criticism suggests that the media does not fulfil its role of educating the public since it is selective in the information which it provides and how this is presented. This is especially of concern if media owners or editors concentrate on trivia at the expense of key issues of national or international concern.

Editorial freedom

A third criticism which has been directed against the media is concerned with its editorial freedom: should the media be free to publish any story which it believes is of interest to the general public? Censorship is regarded as an anathema to a liberal democratic system of government. This is suggestive of state control and implies that the media functions as a propaganda tool of the government, as was the case, for example, in the old state of East Germany. Written constitutions in liberal democracies frequently incorporate provisions to guarantee the freedom of the press: the first amendment to the American Constitution contains such a statement and this principle is also enshrined in the German Basic Law.

However, restrictions on the media exist in all liberal democratic systems of government. For example, it is a requirement that reports should be truthful. Those which are not might be subject to actions for slander or libel. A more contentious restriction concerns state interests. Legislation (such as Britain's 1989 Official Secrets Act) is designed to protect the state against subversive activities waged by foreign governments. In Ireland the 1939 Offences Against the State Act or the 1960 Broadcasting Act may be used to prohibit media coverage of the activities of illegal organisations.

However, state interests are difficult to define precisely. Should they cover activities performed by a government in the name of the state which it might find politically embarrassing if revealed to the general public or to world opinion? This issue arose in West Germany in the 1960s in connection with the 'Speigel Affair'. It led to an amendment of the West German criminal code in 1968 whereby the press could be punished for revealing secrets which were clearly and unambiguously a threat to the state's external secrecy.

MEDIA REGULATION IN BRITAIN

There are a wide range of formal and informal mechanisms to regulate the media. Public morality is safeguarded in legislation which includes the 1959 Obscene Publications Act, the 1984 Video Recordings Act, the 1994 Public Order and Criminal Justice Act and also through the work performed by the Broadcasting Standards Council, which was put on a statutory footing in 1990, governing both radio and television.

State interests are safeguarded by the 1989 Official Secrets Act: however governments have a range of other means at their disposal to influence the conduct of the media. These include the D-Notice system (which is a procedure designed to stop the reporting of certain security matters). The political concerns of a government may be furthered through the

> provision of information to selected journalists through the 'lobby system'. Allegations have also been made that appointments to bodies such as the British Broadcasting Corporation and the Independent Television Commission may be used in a partisan manner.

A further contentious area is that of individual privacy. The media's watchdog function may involve publishing information which infringes on the personal life of a public figure. Such information may be obtained in dubious ways including the use of telephoto lenses or bugging devices. This reveals an important dilemma: where does the public's 'right to know' stop and a public person's 'right to privacy' begin?

This issue is often determined by the media themselves who may operate some form of code of practice. However, accusations that the British media, and especially the newspaper industry, has unduly infringed on the privacy of members of the Royal Family and leading politicians has led to calls for the enactment of legislation (in the form of a privacy law) to impose restrictions on the activities of the media. Such would make intrusive behaviour by the newspapers a specific criminal offence. This course of action was rejected by the British government in 1995 although the Press Complaints Commission was given the power to fine editors who breached the industry's Code of Practice.

The media and the conduct of politics

In what ways does the media affect the manner in which the political affairs of a nation are transacted?

In all liberal democracies the media exerts a profound influence over the conduct of political affairs. In the nineteenth century, the only way members of the general public could see leading politicians was to physically attend meetings which they addressed. It followed, therefore, that oratory was a prized political skill in that period. But this is no longer the case. Initially the popular press made it possible for politicians to put their cases to a wider audience than was able to attend a political meeting. Then the radio and now television has enabled leading politicians to address us directly in our own living rooms. This has had a significant influence over the conduct of national election campaigns.

ELECTION CAMPAIGNS

Election campaigns may fulfil one of three roles: they may reinforce a voter's existing loyalty to a political party or attempt to activate its existing supporters to turn out and vote on election day. Alternatively they seek to convert members of the general public and thus gain new sources of electoral support for the party.

Campaigns at national level now utilise technology and market research techniques. Computerised mailing lists, opinion polls and advertising are commonly utilised in an attempt to 'sell' candidates to the general public. These developments, coupled with the enhanced role of the media, particularly television, are costly. In America it has been estimated that $1 billion was expended on all elections held in 1992.

Political meetings are now a less important feature of election campaigns. Politicians seize opportunities offered by the media to project themselves to the electorate: the photo opportunity, the walkabout, the press conference, televised debates and political broadcasts have diminished the importance of the old-style political meeting. The role of the media is especially enhanced in countries such as America in which it is possible for politicians and political parties to buy air time.

Television in particular has had a number of consequences for the conduct of national elections. This provides candidates with an opportunity to address large audiences and 'head to head' televised debates are common in countries with directly elected presidents. In 1995 an estimated audience of over 30 million people listened to the televised debate between Jacques Chirac and Lionel Jospin which was held before the final ballot in the French presidential election.

Even in countries such as Britain with a parliamentary executive, television has tended to focus attention on party leaders and thus transform general elections into contests for the office of prime minister. In such countries, national elections have become 'presidentialised'. Central control over party affairs has been enhanced by this development which has also tended to reduce the importance of activities performed by local party members in connection with the election of candidates to public office.

Additionally, television has placed emphasis on presentation: major political events such as campaign rallies are carefully orchestrated so that viewers are presented with an image of a united and enthusiastic party. Leading politicians are carefully schooled in television techniques since the ability to perform professionally on television has become an essential political skill. Advertising companies play an ever-increasing role in 'selling' political parties and their leaders. The danger with such developments is that content may be of secondary importance to what advertisers refer to as 'packaging'.

However, the influence of the media over the conduct of politics is not confined to national elections. The role performed by legislatures may also be adversely affected. Investigative journalism may provide more effective scrutiny of the actions of the executive than a legislator's speeches or questions. An appearance by a legislator in a brief televised interview will reach a wider audience than a speech delivered within the legislature. One response to the latter issue has been the televising of the proceedings of legislative bodies. The Australian parliament, for example, voted to televise the proceedings of the Senate, House of Representatives and their committees in October 1991.

TELEVISING THE BRITISH HOUSE OF COMMONS

Legislatures may respond to arguments that the media has taken over their traditional functions by using it to publicise their activities. In 1989 the House of Commons allowed its proceedings to be televised. The main benefit intended from this course of action was to make government more visible to members of the general public who would thus understand the importance of the work performed by Parliament. Although the viewing public of live proceedings is not substantial, snippets of broadcasts are utilised in the more widely viewed news programmes.

However, there have also been disadvantages associated with this development. It has been argued that MPs 'play up' to the cameras, perhaps tailoring their speeches to include words or phrases which are likely to get reported. Such are referred to as 'sound bites'. Ministers have also been accused of 'planting' questions: this involves an MP from the government party tabling a question of which the minister has prior knowledge.

This is designed to make the minister appear an effective parliamentary performer on television, thus enhancing the minister's and the government's reputation.

The political influence of the media

Does the media possess the ability to influence the outcome of political events?

Issues such as ownership and bias in the media are regarded as important in liberal democracies as it is assumed that the media possesses considerable ability to determine the course of political events. In this section we consider various arguments concerning the influence of the media on political affairs.

Agenda setting

It is argued that the media has the ability to 'set the political agenda': that is, the media may publicise a particular issue in the hope of concentrating the attention of its readers, listeners or viewers on this topic. Whether this is a good or a bad development depends on the motives which lay behind the media's attempts to influence public perceptions. A beneficial aspect of this activity is that the media may lead public opinion in a progressive direction, perhaps securing action on a social problem which would otherwise have been ignored. In Britain, a television programme shown in 1966, *Cathy Come Home*, had a significant impact on publicising the plight of Britain's homeless and aided the growth of the organisation Shelter.

Alternatively, however, the media may be guided by partisan motives. Attention may be directed at an issue in order to secure support for a course of action favoured by its owner or by the political interests which the owner supports. This may involve whipping up public hysteria to persuade governments to act in a manner advocated by the media or the interests which lay behind it.

'MORAL PANICS'

Moral panics occur when the media concentrates on a particular problem which is exaggerated and blown out of all proportion. This problem is depicted as being typical of a wider social malaise which threatens social tranquillity. It frequently involves groups being made scapegoats and blamed for all of the ills facing society. In undertaking such activities the media are accused of acting at the behest of the powerful interests in society who are threatened by this underlying crisis.

Moral panics often form an aspect of law and order policy, in which the police and courts will be urged by the media to take tough action against a problem, frequently identified with youths. The consequence of moral panics is to produce a more heavily regulated society. This activity is consistent with a Marxist interpretation of the role of the media: it holds that the media is an ideological tool which operates in the interests of the powerful and thereby helps to sustain their position within society. Pluralists ascribe the media a greater degree of independence in a society in which groups and interests compete for power, possibly using the media to advance their concerns.

Reinforcement or change?

Agenda setting is, however, only one aspect of media influence. It is sometimes argued that the media has the ability to determine not merely the policies which governments adopt but, more fundamentally, their political complexion. This accusation implies that the media has a significant influence over voting behaviour at election times. There are two basic schools of thought concerning the ability of the media to influence how we vote. The debate centres on the extent to which the media merely reinforces existing political behaviour rather than is able to act as the agent of political change.

Those who argue that the media reinforces existing political activity suggest that the power of the media over politics is limited since most members of the general public have preconceived political opinions. They will either read, listen or view material which is consistent with these existing ideas or ignore contrary ideas should these be expressed. Further, as the media knows the tastes of its clientele, it will cater for these opinions and not run the risk of losing readers, listeners or viewers. The reinforcement theory thus suggests that issues of media bias are of no significant political importance even at election times.

A contrary opinion to the reinforcement theory suggests that the media has a profound influence over political activity such as voting behaviour. It is suggested that many people are unaware of the political biases of the media to which they are subject and may thus be influenced by the manner in which it portrays events, especially when such exposure takes place over a long period of time.

This may be especially important when the gap between the leading parties for political office is small: the British Conservative Party's election victory in 1992 has been attributed to the influence exerted by the Conservative tabloid press on undecided voters, and Silvio Berlusconi's victory in the 1994 Italian elections has been explained by the impact of his three television channels on voting behaviour.

MEDIA INFLUENCE OVER POLITICAL EVENTS

It is alleged that the role of the media extends beyond merely influencing the outcome of elections: it also may promote major political episodes.

In Britain it was alleged that the Social Democratic Party (formed in 1981) was a media creation. This argument suggested that the heavy emphasis placed in the media on ideological divisions within the Labour Party was a major factor in inducing a number of social democrats to form a new political vehicle to advance their views.

The initial successes enjoyed by that party were also attributed to media interest in that party's affairs – an interest which waned when the Falklands War commenced in 1982.

The extent to which the media influences political affairs is thus open to debate. It is one social agency among other several others (such as the family, the workplace or the neighbourhood) which may affect political conduct. Those without established political views or loyalties (who are described as 'don't knows' in opinion polls) may be most susceptible to media influence.

The suggestion that the media can influence the political behaviour of at least some members of the general public thus implies that issues such as ownership and political bias are important in a liberal democracy. It may mean that some parties have an unfair advantage over others.

Cross-media ownership

What does the term 'cross-media ownership' mean and why is this of relevance to the conduct of politics?

Traditionally media operations were discrete: a 'separation of media powers' existed in many liberal democracies whereby ownership of the print media was divorced from other major forms of communication such as radio and television. While it became increasingly common in the twentieth century for newspaper ownership to be concentrated in relatively few hands by a process of mergers, such processes were conducted within the print media. But this is now changing. Increasingly media owners have financial interests in various forms of communication including newspapers, journals, radio and television. This is what we mean by 'cross-media ownership'. In the remainder of this section we consider why this development occurred and what problems might arise as the result of it.

The development of cross-media ownership

The role of the private sector in ownership of television companies has had a profound influence on this development. In many European countries television was initially viewed as a form of public service. It was operated by the state (sometimes using the mechanism of public corporations) whose main duty was to ensure that news was reported in an impartial fashion: objectivity and balance were the guiding principles of public service broadcasting.

The monopoly enjoyed by public service broadcasting was eventually challenged by the private sector who sought to make a profit from this form of communication. This gave rise to commercial television which was exclusively funded by advertising revenue (unlike public service broadcasting which was mainly funded by its users paying a licence fee, sometimes, as in West Germany, topped up by income derived from advertising). The costs involved in establishing a television channel made it essential that established business and commercial interests should involve themselves in commercial television. In many countries, however, commercial broadcasting was initially subject to state supervision. This was justified on the grounds that the frequencies available for transmission were limited in number and so the state had to regulate the use of this scarce commodity.

However, more recent developments concerned especially with cable and satellite television have facilitated a massive growth in the number of television channels which can be transmitted within any one particular country. Although these may also be subject to some degree of state supervision (cable and satellite channels in Britain, for example, are loosely regulated by the Independent Television Commission) these innovations have served to further increase the role of the private sector in broadcasting.

Problems associated with cross-media ownership

Cable and satellite channels are attractive to the private sector whose role in broadcasting has been further facilitated by the process of deregulation: this occurred in Italy and France in particular, during the 1980s. Many of these commercial and business interests were already engaged in other aspects of media activity such as newspapers and radio. The ability of an individual or a commercial company to have interests in a wide range of media outlets has considerable political significance.

One major problem is that such media owners possess a considerable degree of power: as we have described above, they may seek to place ideas on the political agenda or to influence the manner in which members of the general public think or act. Their ability to do so may be enhanced by a situation in which a wide range of media outlets hammer out a common political line.

Cross-ownership may further erode the very diversity of the media which is regarded as essential in a liberal democracy. It is important that the media articulates a wide range of opinions in order for members of the public to become politically educated. A similarity of views expressed in various media forms may be more reminiscent of a one-party state than of a society which flourishes on the expression of a variety of opinions.

A further difficulty with cross-ownership is that commercial concerns dominate the content of newspapers or programmes. A major fear is that stories or programmes will cater for the lowest common denominator. While this problem may seem confined to media operating on commercial lines it has serious implications for public service broadcasting. If they lose viewers to commercial television companies their case for receiving all, or any, of a licence fee paid by the public is undermined.

However, it would be incorrect to assume that all developments in the media have consequences for the conduct of politics which are undesirable. Innovations which include desktop publishing, cable and satellite broadcasting do theoretically facilitate a diversity of opinion which is beneficial to a healthy liberal democracy. New media ventures (such as Ted Turner's Cable News Network) have succeeded and a wide range of additional broadcasting outlets have been created, eroding the power previously enjoyed by media 'giants'. In America, for example, the power previously enjoyed by ABC, CBS and NBC has been broken and one feature of the 1992 Presidential election campaign was the enhanced role of local cable television stations.

The key consideration is the extent to which companies taking advantage of these developments are able to remain independent. Developments in the mid-1990s in connection with the Information Superhighway has tended to promote take-overs and mergers resulting in the formation of large companies with diverse media interests. If small companies are taken over or driven out of business by larger concerns with interests in a range of different forms of communication the benefits which could be derived from technological innovations will be lost. It is this concern which has prompted the enactment of national or state legislation to limit the extent of cross-media ownership.

THE REGULATION OF MEDIA OWNERSHIP IN BRITAIN

Mergers within the newspaper industry affecting large operations have required the consent of the Secretary of State since 1965, who may refer the matter to the Monopolies Commission. But consent to such activities is the norm. In 1981, for example, Rupert Murdoch was allowed to purchase *The Times* and *The Sunday Times*, giving him a large share of the national daily and Sunday newspaper market. But Rupert

Murdoch's interests went beyond newspapers. He owned a cable television company, Sky Cable Company, which merged with British Satellite Broadcasting in 1991 to form B Sky B.

In some countries (such as Australia and America) restrictions have been imposed on such cross-media ownership. In Britain, the 1981 Broadcasting Act prevented newspapers from owning independent television companies, but this provision did not extend to cable television. This matter was considered in a 1995 Green Paper. The 1995 Broadcasting Bill proposed to allow national newspapers to own independent television companies (with the exception of Rupert Murdoch's News International and Mirror Group Newspapers) and for television companies to take over newspapers.

Questions

1 Provide and comment upon two examples of the way in which the media is an aid to the functioning of liberal democratic forms of government.
2 'The media should be free to publish whatever it thinks necessary: there should be no restrictions placed on its operations'. Provide three reasoned arguments against this proposition.
3 With reference to any country with which you are familiar, indicate two benefits and two disadvantages which have occurred as the result of the attention devoted by television to national election campaigns.
4 What is 'cross-media ownership'? Provide two reasons why this is sometimes regarded as a problem which liberal democracies need to address.

Summary

1 The media is an important source of information on current affairs and political events. This aids the operations of liberal democracy by:
   • facilitating public involvement in policy making;
   • enhancing the ability of governments to be held accountable for their actions.

2 Some problems are associated with the workings of the media.
These include:
- some sections of the media (especially the press) are not
impartial and may seek to indoctrinate public opinion to the
benefit of one particular political party;
- the media is selective in the information it provides: some issues
may be ignored as they lack 'newsworthiness';
- the reporting freedom of the media may require curtailing (for
example on the grounds of state secrecy or to safeguard an
individual's privacy).

3 The media has exerted a major influence over the conduct of the
political affairs in liberal democracies:
- television has exerted a major influence over the conduct of
elections;
- the media may have the ability to 'agenda set' that is, to direct
the attention of citizens to selected issues: there may be
underlying political motives governing this activity;
- voting behaviour may be influenced by the media, especially by
the partisan press: there is, however, debate concerning whether
the press reinforces existing political habits or can act as an
agent of change.

4 The broadcasting media (especially in Europe) has increasingly
been subject to involvement by the private sector and this has been
intensified by deregulation of state broadcasting organisations and
by the advent of cable and satellite television.
A particular concern has been 'cross-media ownership' in which
one individual or company has interests in a diverse range of
media operations (such as newspapers, radio and television).

7

CONSTITUTIONS

Definition

What is a constitution? Why do states have them?

As students of politics we need to know how a country's system of government operates. For example we may wish to ascertain what power is possessed by head of state. Or we may be interested in the relationship between the executive and the legislature or between the government and its citizens. We would turn to a constitution to discover information of this nature.

A constitution sets a framework within which a country's system of government is conducted. It establishes rules which those who exercise the functions of government have to obey. All future actions performed by the executive and legislature, for example, must be in conformity with the country's constitutional provisions.

There is usually one document which contains information concerning the manner in which a country's system of government operates. Examples of such codified documents include the American constitution which was drawn up in 1787, the Irish constitution of 1937 and the French constitution of 1958. The provisions of codified constitutions have a superior status to ordinary legislation and provide a key point of reference whereby the activities performed by the executive and legislative branches of government can be judged. Actions which contravene it may be set aside by the process of judicial review. Britain and New Zealand, alternatively, are examples of countries which do not have codified constitutions.

However, it would be impossible to include all the material relevant to the government of a country in one single document. Codified constitutions are supplemented by several additional sources to provide detailed information concerning the operations of a country's system of government. A constitution sometimes establishes broad principles of action whose detailed implementation is left to legislation. Such statutes constitute a further source of information concerning the manner in which government functions. Other sources include declarations made by judges whose work may involve interpreting the constitution. These written sources are supplemented by the adoption of practices concerning the way in which government works. These latter are usually termed conventions.

CONVENTIONS

The manner in which a country's system of government operates is often determined by customs or practices rather than by specific constitutional enactment. Such constitutional conventions may fundamentally alter arrangements contained or implied in a country's constitution.

The 1958 French constitution gave the National Assembly the power to dismiss prime ministers. However, their willingness to accept that they could be dismissed by the president even when enjoying the support of the legislature facilitated the extension of the president's power. The American constitution envisaged that Congress would be the main source of legislation. In practice, however, the president subsequently assumed a major role in initiating legislation.

Codified constitutions are traditionally drawn up following some major political event or crisis which necessitates the reconstruction of the apparatus of government. There is a widely felt need to 'start afresh'. In America new arrangements for government were required when this country secured her independence from Britain in the late eighteenth century. A similar situation required an Irish constitution to be written following the First World War. In Italy and the old state of West Germany, defeat in war and the collapse of fascism necessitated the construction of new governing arrangements. In France the Algerian war provided the occasion for the drafting of a new constitution in 1958, thus bringing the Fifth Republic into being.

The role of a constitution

What do we learn from studying a country's constitution?

The key features of government

A constitution describes the essential features of a country's system of government. A constitution contains a formal statement of the composition of the key branches of government – the legislature, executive and the judiciary – and refers to the role which each of these play in the machinery of government.

THE COMPOSITION OF AMERICAN GOVERNMENT

The American constitution provided for a legislature which is termed 'Congress'. It consists of two chambers – the House of Representatives and the Senate. The constitution allocated the executive function to the president while the judicial function was ascribed to a supreme court and a range of subordinate courts. This constitution further stipulated the qualifications required for membership of the House of Representatives and the Senate and laid down conditions governing the presidency, including eligibility to serve in that office and the length of that official's tenure.

The functions of each branch of government were also discussed in this document. A key role given to Congress was that of levying and collecting taxes. One duty allocated to the president was to be commander-in-chief of the country's armed forces. The federal judiciary was charged with upholding federal law, including the constitution, and arbitrating disputes between two or more states.

A constitution further informs us of the relationship between the branches of government. The American president, for example, is required to periodically deliver a state of the union address to Congress and may put forward legislative proposals for that body's consideration.

Citizens' rights

In liberal democracies we usually find statements contained in constitutions concerning the relationship between the government and its citizens. Such documents typically contain safeguards against arbitrary conduct by a government which are designed to safeguard individual freedom. The German constitution, for example, contains a prominent statement of basic rights which guarantee its citizens a range of personal freedoms. The omission of such provisions was regarded as a major weakness of the American constitution. Accordingly ten amendments (collectively known as the Bill of Rights) were incorporated into this document in 1791.

THE AMERICAN BILL OF RIGHTS

The first ten amendments to the American constitution list a range of personal freedoms. These include the freedom of religion, speech and assembly and the right to petition for the redress of grievances. The constitution safeguards the freedom of all citizens to possess arms. Provisions concerning the manner in which citizens or their property can be searched are incorporated into this document which also establishes the right of an accused person to a speedy and public trial.

Similar provisions are found in many other constitutions. In Ireland, personal rights such as the equality of all citizens before the law, the right of habeas corpus and the freedom of expression (including the right to criticise government policy) are embodied into the constitution. In Italy the right to join a political party or a trade union is enshrined in such a document.

Traditionally such freedoms primarily concerned the conduct of political affairs and the operations of the criminal justice system. They were designed to prevent governments acting in an overbearing fashion towards its citizens. In the late twentieth century, however, other forms of rights have entered political debates. These include social rights such as the right to a job, the right to be housed, the right to enjoy a minimum standard of living or the right for a woman to have an abortion. Although legislation may sometimes remove impediments to prevent specific groups of citizens from exercising defined social functions, constitutions rarely contain any fundamental, all-embracing statement of social rights.

Guarantor of a federal system of government

In a federal country in which government is jointly exercised by national and sub-national units, the constitution will commonly establish the division of responsibilities which exists within that country between these units. The existence of these sub-national bodies is guaranteed by the constitution.

The balance of power between the federal and state governments in America, for example, is discussed in the constitution, especially in the tenth amendment which stipulates that powers not expressly delegated to the federal government in that document nor prohibited from being exercised by the states would be 'reserved to the states respectively, or to the people'. We shall discuss the changing nature of the balance between federal and state governments in America in Chapter 12.

UNCONSTITUTIONAL AND ANTI-CONSTITUTIONAL ACTIONS

An unconstitutional act is one which contravenes either the letter or the spirit of the constitution. The perpetrator usually contravenes one specific constitutional provision or convention. In Britain a government refusing to resign following the passage of a 'no confidence' motion in the House of Commons would be accused of acting unconstitutionally.

An anti-constitutional action is one which displays a total disregard for the entire constitutional arrangements which exist within a particular country and may seek to overthrow them. The assassination of the Israeli prime minister, Yitzhak Rabin, in 1995 in an attempt to alter the direction of government policy towards the Palestinians, was an example of an anti-constitutional action. Military intervention to overthrow a system of liberal democracy and impose a different form of government is a further example. The overthrow of Salvador Allende's government in Chile in 1973 and its replacement by a military regime headed by General Pinochet was an anti-constitutional action.

The embodiment of political values

A constitution will tell us about the political views and values of those who wrote it. The Italian constitution of 1947 reveals a desire on the part of its authors to organise that country's system of government in order to prevent the return of fascism. This was reflected in the widespread dispersal of political power and the absence of a provision for the direct election of the president. The French constitution of 1958 displayed a commitment by its authors that strong, effective government was an essential guarantee of national security. They sought to secure this objective by strengthening the executive branch at the expense of the legislature. Parties such as the socialists who traditionally viewed a strong legislature as the essence of republicanism subsequently accepted the enhanced power of the presidency. The transitional arrangements in the South African constitution providing for power sharing at all levels of government (until majority rule is established in 1999) indicates a desire to protect the interests of the white minority in the formative years of the new Republic.

An examination of a constitution thus enables us to discover how theory is translated into practice and how the climate of political opinion at the time of that document's drafting subsequently influenced the conduct of a country's governing institutions. It thus embodies a statement of political theory and political history. We shall examine this situation more fully in relationship to the drafting of the American Constitution.

The principles of the American Constitution

The 55 delegates who assembled at Philadelphia in 1787 to draft the American constitution were influenced by a variety of political ideas and priorities. These included John Locke's social contract theory and Montesquieu's concept of the separation of powers.

The separation of powers was advocated by Montesquieu in his work *De l'Esprit des lois*, written in 1748. This held that tyranny was most effectively avoided if the three branches of government (the legislature, executive and judiciary) were separate. This implied that each branch would possess a degree of autonomy and its personnel should be different. This theory appealed to those who drafted the American constitution. It was widely believed that George III's unreasonable treatment of the American colonists had triggered the war of independence in 1775. The monarch embodied all three functions of government and was thus prone to tyrannical action.

Accordingly the constitution placed the legislative, executive and judicial functions of government into the hands of different bodies. The legislature consisted of House of Representatives and the Senate, the executive was placed in the hands of the president, and the judicial function of national government was placed in the hands of justices of the supreme court and judges of subordinate courts. Many subsequent constitutions have adopted this principle to a greater or lesser extent.

However, it was also accepted that total autonomy exercised by the three branches of government could be prejudicial to the rights and liberties of the people. In an extreme form, three tyrannies might be substituted for one. Accordingly the American constitution deliberately instituted procedures in which the workings of one branch of government could be affected or influenced by the operations of another. This is known as checks and balances. An example of this concerns the relationship between Congress and the president in the area of law making. According to the constitution, laws passed by Congress have to be subsequently agreed by the president. If the president is not satisfied with the content of a bill, it may be vetoed. However, Congress may override this veto provided that two-thirds of the members of both Houses support this action. It was anticipated that these procedures would avoid unreasonable action being undertaken by the legislative or executive branches of government.

The main problem with a system of checks and balances is that it can result in inertia – the involvement of numerous people in decision making may result in nothing being done as one group effectively cancels out the work of another.

A codified constitution as a living document

How do codified constitutions survive over long periods of time?

Codified constitutions are designed to be enduring documents. The process of drafting and ratifying a constitution is a lengthy one. No country can thus afford the luxury of frequently re-writing its constitution.

The question we need to address, therefore, is how can a document written at one specific point in time endure for many years after. In particular we shall consider how a constitution can adjust to subsequent social, economic and political changes which may have a significant impact on the role and operations of government and how it might it respond to eventualities which were not perceived when the document was originally drawn up.

The process of amendment

Constitutions generally contain provisions whereby additions or deletions can be made to the original document. The mechanics of the amending process, however, is subject to great variation. Flexible constitutions are those which can be amended by the normal law-making process. The uncodified British constitution (discussed below) is a good example of a flexible constitution, but the German constitution can also be altered by the normal law-making process.

AMENDMENT OF THE GERMAN CONSTITUTION

Changes to the German constitution are constrained by two factors. One is that they must secure the support of at least two-thirds of the members of both the *Bundestag* and the *Bundesrat*. The other is that certain elements of the constitution cannot be amended. These concern the key principles governing the operations of the state, including its 'democratic and social' nature, the ability of the people to exercise political power through the process of voting in elections and the functioning of government through legislative, executive and judicial organs. The role performed by the states (*Länder*) in the process of government may also not be altered.

Usually, however, constitutions can be amended only by a process which is separate from the normal law making process utilised in a particular country. These are termed rigid constitutions.

RIGID CONSTITUTIONS – IRELAND AND AMERICA

Amendment of the Irish constitution requires that a referendum must be held to determine popular support or rejection for any constitutional change put forward by Parliament (the *Oireachtas*). Examples of amendments which were made using such a procedure included two in connection with Ireland's membership of the European Union (in 1972 and 1987).

The American constitution can be amended in two ways. The manner which is usually utilised requires two-thirds of the members of both Houses of Congress to approve a change, following which it is submitted to state legislatures or ratification conventions organised at state level. A proposal needs the support of three-quarters of the states in order to be incorporated into the constitution. The alternative method enables the states rather than Congress to initiate the process of reform.

Amendments provide one obvious way for a constitution to be kept up to date. Those made to the American constitution include civil rights issues such as the abolition of slavery, the right of women to vote and the universal introduction of votes at the age of 18. The power of federal government was enhanced by the amendment which authorised Congress to levy income tax.

Generally amendments are most easily secured to flexible constitutions. When the amending process is lengthy and drawn out changes become more difficult. There have only been 26 amendments made to the American constitution since 1789. Well-supported changes (such as the Equal Rights Amendment in the 1970s) failed to secure sufficient support to be incorporated into that document. One potential danger with rigid constitutions is that they fail to keep abreast of social changes.

Judicial review

A second way whereby constitutions can be adapted to suit changed circumstances is through the process of judicial review. Many codified constitutions give this function to the judiciary. In performing this function judges may draw solely on their legal expertise or they may, as in the case in Germany, consider submissions from interested parties before reaching a judgment. Judicial review enables the courts to inject contemporary views and values into a country's constitution when they are required to deliver judgment on a specific issue which comes before them. Judicial review may extend the scope of state activity or it may affect a citizen's civil rights. The American supreme court's decision (in *'Roe'* v. *Wade*, 1973) that under certain circumstances a woman had a right to an abortion is an example of judicial interpretation of the constitution.

THE GERMAN CONSTITUTION AND COMMERCIAL BROADCASTING

The development of commercial broadcasting in the former state of West Germany illustrates the importance of judicial review in restraining the actions of government but also the ability of the courts to adjust their interpretation of the constitution in line with changing attitudes and values.

In 1961 the Constitutional Court rejected the attempt by Chancellor Adenauer's government to set up a national commercial television channel. Ten years later the Court upheld the independence of public service broadcasting by preventing the federal government from subjecting the licence fee to VAT. However, in 1981 the Court permitted broadcasting to expand as the result of cable and satellite technologies and in 1986 gave its blessing to a private commercial sector existing alongside the public service sector. In 1987 the balance between these two sectors was detailed in five separate rulings of the Court.

Judicial review is most easily facilitated when the constitution lacks precision. Constitutions frequently contain statements of principle. These embody the spirit of the constitution. Such declarations institute values to be observed henceforth. Generalised principles may set the tone for subsequent judicial interpretations when specific activities come before the courts for adjudication. In such a manner the constitution may validly be applied to situations and events which were not envisaged when the original document was written. All that is required is to apply its principles to new and changed conditions.

There are two dangers with the process of interpretation. The first is when the core values enshrined in this document lose their appeal because broader social changes make them unfashionable. In such circumstances the constitution may lose its authority and under extreme circumstances may have to be replaced by a new document.

The second problem is that an acceptance that the constitution is a document whose meaning is variable and determined by judicial interpretation may result in the loss of its ability to restrain the actions of government. The ability to adjust a constitution in this manner may result in sanction being given to any action which the government wishes to undertake, especially when the latter has some ability to determine the personnel of the courts. The constitution does not, therefore, meaningfully limit the operations of government or force it to subscribe to any basic standard of behaviour as it ceases to be an independent source of power which is essential if it to act as an impartial arbitrator.

Britain's uncodified constitution

Where can information concerning Britain's constitution be found?

Britain possesses an uncodified constitution. With the exception of the Commonwealth period, 1649–60, there has been no political revolution or fundamental political crisis to justify the writing of a constitution. The processes of government have been subject to evolutionary adjustments enabling them to accommodate major changes including the agricultural and industrial revolutions in the eighteenth and nineteenth centuries and the expanded role of the state after 1945. There is thus no one document which provides a basic store of knowledge concerning the operations of the branches of government or the rights and liberties of the subject in Britain. Instead information of the type normally contained in a constitution is dispersed. There are a wide range of written and unwritten sources to the British constitution.

The sources of Britain's constitution

Statute law
There are numerous examples of Acts of Parliament which govern the way in which Britain's system of government operates. Examples include the 1911 and 1949 Parliament Acts (which concern the

relationship between the House of Commons and the House of Lords and which specify the powers of the latter chamber) and the 1971 Courts Act (which established the present system of Crown Courts).

European law

Britain's membership of the European Community in 1972 involved the incorporation of the European Convention, the Treaties of Rome and 43 volumes of existing European legislation into British law. These provisions and subsequent European legislation perform an important role in determining the operation of Britain's system of government.

Judicial interpretation

Traditionally the British courts lacked the power to declare Parliament's statutes null and void on the grounds that their contents contravened provisions of the constitution. The process of judicial review was solely concerned with determining whether powers derived from statute or common law had been correctly applied. However, Britain's membership of the European Union involves the courts determining whether Parliament's legislation is compatible with European law which has precedence.

Common law

Common law derives from historic customs and traditions whose principles have been enshrined in case law developed by judges since the Norman Conquest. Many of the liberties of the subject (such as the freedoms of assembly, speech, movement and privacy) are rooted in common law.

Conventions

Many matters concerning the operations of government are governed by practices which have become the accepted way of behaving. One example of this concerns ministerial responsibility which governs the relationship between the executive and legislative branches of government. One advantage of a convention is that it can be disregarded if circumstances justify this course of action. Harold Wilson's suspension of the principle of collective ministerial responsibility during the referendum campaign on Britain's continued membership of the European Economic Community in 1975 was an example of political expediency overriding normal constitutional practice.

MINISTERIAL RESPONSIBILITY IN BRITAIN

There are two types of ministerial responsibility. Individual ministerial responsibility concerns the relationship between ministers and the departments which they control. As the political head of a department ministers are expected to be accountable for all actions which it undertakes. If a serious error is committed by that department, the minister may be required to resign. This convention does not apply to ministers who resign (or who are forced to resign) as the result of some form of personal indiscretion. It is solely concerned with the formal role which they occupy within a department.

Collective ministerial responsibility embraces the relationship of the entire executive branch to the legislature. It is assumed that major issues of policy, even if associated with one specific department, have been discussed at cabinet level and thus constitute overall government policy. There are two consequences of this. First, ministers are collectively accountable to the House of Commons for all items of government policy. Theirs is a 'one out, all out' relationship. A vote of 'no confidence' in the government requires the resignation of all of its members. Second, while a minister has the right to voice opinions on an issue discussed within the Cabinet, once a decision has been reached it is binding on all of its participants. A minister who is not in agreement with what has been decided should either resign or 'toe the line' and be prepared to publicly defend the outcome which has been reached.

The case for constitution reform in Britain

Why has the need for constitutional reform been put forward in Britain in recent years?

The lack of a codified constitution is of profound significance. With the exception of European legislation there is no constitutional enactment superior to ordinary statute law. Other sources of the constitution are ultimately subordinate to this. Accordingly, the constitution is whatever Parliament decrees it to be. This has significant implications for the conduct of government. The actions taken by Parliament (and the government which exercises control over it) is constrained only by adherence to popular conceptions as to what is correct behaviour. The restraints which Britain's constitution imposes on the workings of government are thus spiritual rather than legalistic.

Within this general context specific arguments have been put forward in recent years to justify constitutional reform which we discuss below.

The operations of the institutions of government

Britain is a unitary state with political power concentrated in national political institutions. The centralised nature of the British state and its alleged neglect of the impact of issues such as industrial decline and unemployment have often been cited as explanations for the periodic interest in national Parliaments for Scotland and Wales. Such would involve the devolution of power from Whitehall and Westminster and the creation of centres of decision making away from London.

The workings of the courts have also been criticised. The media frequently highlights what is depicted as judicial shortcomings. The main problem concerns the relative freedom which judges enjoy from political accountability. This grants them a wide degree of autonomy. Although this may be justified (since it prevents governments applying direct pressure onto the judiciary to secure verdicts which it favours) it might enable gender, race or class prejudices to influence judicial decisions.

Executive domination of the legislature

A second criticism which has been put forward to justify constitutional reform has been directed at the relations between the branches of government, particularly between the executive and legislature. Politicians of a variety of political persuasions have periodically decried the power of the executive. In 1976 Lord Hailsham referred to an 'elective dictatorship', while during the 1980s the apparent emergence of a 'one-party state' led many Labour politicians to question the situation in which a political party could continually secure office with the support of a minority of the voting public.

Various reforms have been suggested to remedy this situation. These include devolution, reforming the House of Lords, changing the voting system or placing some form of limitation on the power of Parliament through a written constitution.

The erosion of individual freedoms

A third reason for the emergence of constitutional reform onto Britain's political agenda has been the perception that individual freedoms have been eroded, especially by the actions of the executive. Groups such as Charter 88 have voiced such concerns. During the 1970s a number of innovations took place in Northern Ireland which curtailed civil liberties. These included legislation such as the Emergency Provisions Act and the introduction of Crown Court trials without juries. During the 1980s further developments occurred elsewhere in the United Kingdom. Legislation such as the 1986 Public Order Act placed restrictions on the ability of individuals to protest and express dissent. The 1994 Public Order and Criminal Justice Act eroded the right to silence which many saw as a cardinal feature of the English criminal justice system. Henceforth the refusal by an accused person to answer questions put by the police might be drawn to the attention of the jury by a trial judge.

A range of measures passed in the 1980s had a profound effect on trade union organisation and activity by placing restrictions on many of the 'rights' previously exercised by such bodies and their members in key areas such as striking and picketing. Such organisations were banned from the Government Communications Headquarters in 1984 implying a belief that unions were subversive organisations.

A Bill of Rights or a written constitution

It has been argued that the defence of individual rights would most readily be facilitated by the enactment of a Bill of Rights. This would put citizens' rights on a statutory basis and make it more difficult for the executive branch to restrict them. One way to secure such a reform would be to incorporate the European Convention of Human Rights into British law. Some politicians have suggested a more fundamental reform and have proposed that Britain should possess a written (or codified) constitution.

THE COMMONWEALTH OF BRITAIN BILL

In 1991 the Labour MP, Tony Benn, introduced the Commonwealth of Britain Bill. This sought to transform Britain into a 'democratic, secular, federal Commonwealth, comprising the Nations of England, Scotland and Wales'.

The key provisions of this bill included the establishment of a bicameral legislature (the House of Commons and the House of the People) elected for a fixed term of four years. The prime minister would be elected by the House of Commons and the government would be accountable to that body. The head of state would be a president elected by both Houses of Parliament, who would preside over a Council of State also chosen by these two Houses. A High Court would be responsible for reviewing any administrative act of the executive. The monarchy would be abolished and the Church of England disestablished.

The bill proposed that such provisions should be incorporated into a written constitution which would be subject to popular approval in a referendum.

Apart from the fact that codified constitutions are usually produced following a major political upheaval, there are many practical objections voiced against such a reform. It is argued that a written constitution would undermine the principle of the sovereignty of Parliament. However, this has already been considerably affected by Britain's entry into the European Community. It is also alleged that a codified constitution would not necessarily ensure that civil rights were more effectively protected. Personal rights rooted in common law may be broader than those contained in a constitutional document. A Bill of Rights as part of a written constitution might thus circumscribe rather than extend these rights.

Further, codified constitutions do not invariably defend civil liberties. Legal discrimination against women persisted for many years in countries such as France despite constitutional provisions seeming to outlaw such practices. The old state of West Germany imposed restrictions on the freedom of speech even though the constitution seemed to prohibit such actions. A final objection to a written constitution concerns the ability of the judiciary to interpret legislation in relation to this document. Although there may be objections to the power exercised by modern executives, it is open to question as to whether the situation would be improved by subjecting actions of the legislature or executive to unelected and politically unaccountable judges.

Questions

1 What is a constitutional convention? With reference to any country with which you are familiar, give some examples of conventions, indicating their significance for the operations of government.
2 Why do countries have constitutions? Are there any essential differences between codified and unwritten constitutions?
3 What do you understand by the term 'checks and balances'? With reference to the constitution of any country with which you are familiar, list some examples of checks and balances.
4 Give some examples of personal freedoms. Is a Bill of Rights incorporated into a codified constitution the best way to ensure that such freedoms are protected?

Summary

1 Constitutions set a framework within which a country's system of government is conducted. Constitutions may be codified ('written') or uncodified ('unwritten'). Codified constitutions enjoy a superior status to that possessed by ordinary legislation and govern the actions of those who exercise functions of government which may be set aside through the process of judicial review. In both cases, however, constitutions are supplemented by other material (such as conventions) which are relevant to the conduct of government.
2 Constitutions contain formal statements concerning the composition of the legislative, executive and judicial branches of government and of the relationships between them. Constitutions frequently include statements of the relationship between government and its citizens, guaranteeing a range of personal freedoms to the latter. In a federal country, constitutions establish a division of power between the national government and its constituent units. Further, as codified constitutions are written at specific historic periods, they inform us of the political views and attitudes of those who drafted them.
3. Constitutions are designed to be enduring documents. They may be kept up to date in two ways. The first of these is the process of amendment. The terms 'flexible' and 'rigid' denote the way in which amendments may be secured. The latter requires a process which is different from the normal law-making procedure but its length and complexity may result in the constitution failing to

keep abreast of social changes. The second of these is the process of judicial review which may affect the scope of governmental activity. One danger with judicial review is that it may prevent the constitution from being an independent arbitrator of the actions undertaken by government.

4 Britain possesses an uncodified constitution. The sources of this include statute law, common law, European law and conventions. However, the absence of a codified document is significant to the conduct of government: with the exception of obligations derived from European legislation, the constitution is effectively whatever the executive (which usually dominates Parliament) decrees it to consist of. Within this general context, arguments have been put forward in recent years for constitutional reform. This would involve either a Bill of Rights or a codified constitution. The latter may be opposed, however, not simply because of its implications for the sovereignty of Parliament but also because it would tend to enhance the power of the judiciary.

8

THE EXECUTIVE BRANCH OF GOVERNMENT

Role

What is the executive branch of government?

The work of the executive branch of government is performed by two distinct sets of people. These are politicians and paid, permanent officials. As we will consider the workings of the bureaucracy in Chapter 9, the discussion here will concentrate on the role performed by politicians within the executive branch of government.

The political control of a state's affairs is under the direction of a broadly-constituted group referred to as 'the government'. For example, in Britain the government consists of the prime minister, cabinet and junior ministers. In America it is composed of the president and the cabinet. Within liberal democracies, governments tend to be either parliamentary or presidential.

A parliamentary system of government is one in which the personnel of government is drawn from the legislature and is located within that body. The government is collectively accountable to the legislature for its actions and remains in office only while it retains the confidence of that body. Countries which include Britain, Germany, Australia and New Zealand have this form of government.

COLLECTIVE MINISTERIAL RESPONSIBILITY

The mechanics of the process of collective ministerial responsibility vary. In Britain, a vote of 'no confidence' in the government by the House of Commons would usually result in the government's resignation and a general election. This situation last occurred in 1979.

To oust a government in Germany, however, the *Bundestag* is required to pass what is known as a 'constructive vote of no confidence'. This entails a vote of no confidence in the chancellor coupled with the selection of a replacement (who is required to obtain an absolute majority vote in the *Bundestag*). This process occurred in 1982 when Chancellor Schmidt was replaced by Chancellor Kohl following the decision of the Free Democrats to form a coalition government with the Christian Democrats.

A presidential system of government is one in which the personnel of the executive and legislative branches are different. They are chosen separately. America possesses this system of government. Neither the president nor other members of the government can be serving members of Congress and the principle of collective responsibility to the legislature does not apply here.

There are, however, hybrid systems which include elements of parliamentary and presidential systems of government. The French system of government is an example of this which we discuss in more detail below.

The French system of government

In France the traditional division which exists between a parliamentary and presidential system of government has been obscured by the emergence of dual leadership within the executive branch of government.

The 1958 constitution established the new office of president with powers additional to those normally associated with a head of state. The president was given a very wide range of functions and powers with which to perform them. These included acting as guarantor of national independence and protecting the functioning of public powers and the continuity of the state. Key duties included appointing the prime minister, presiding over the cabinet, and acting as commander-in-chief of the armed forces. Special emergency powers could also be exercised by the president. The power and prestige of the presidency has grown, especially since direct election was introduced in 1962. The 'monarchical drift' of the office was acknowledged by the new president, Jacques Chirac during the 1995 presidential election. The president serves for a period of seven years and the office is seen as France's key political prize.

The division of power between the president and prime minister is of central importance to an understanding of the operations of the French system of government. A major role of the president is to appoint (and dismiss) the prime minister. A newly appointed prime minister does not have to seek a specific vote of confidence from the National Assembly although he or she is accountable to that body. In making such a choice, however, the president is constrained by the political composition of the National Assembly. It follows, therefore, that the power of the president is greatest when the president's party controls the National Assembly. The prime minister is effectively a presidential nominee which was the case with President Chirac's first appointment to this post, Alain Juppé.

However, if the party affiliation of the president and the majority in the legislature is different, the president is forced to select a prime minister and a government who enjoy the support of the National Assembly. The prime minister is more likely to be assertive in such situations since he or she possesses a separate power base and is not totally reliant on presidential support to obtain or remain in office. This may thus reduce the president's power and occurred between 1986 and 1988 and between 1993 and 1995 when a socialist president (Mitterrand) was forced to coexist with a right wing government dominated by the Gaullists. In such periods of cohabitation, however, a president is far from impotent. Ultimately it is possible to dissolve the legislature. Lionel Jospin (the unsuccessful Socialist candidate in the 1995 presidential election) stated that should he win he would dissolve the National Assembly in the hope of securing a Socialist majority in a general election.

Relations within the executive branch

How is power allocated within the government?

Leadership within the government is exercised by a chief executive. This person appoints other members of the government and usually exercises a pre-eminent position within it, being regarded as the nation's 'leader'.

KEY FUNCTIONS OF THE CHIEF EXECUTIVE

1 The initiation of proposals for government policy. Often these derive from the party's election manifesto, although chief executives are also required to respond to unforseen issues which require the government's attention.

2 Overseeing the administration and execution of policy and the overall conduct of the government. The exercise of this strategic role may mean that the chief executive intervenes in the specific activities performed by individual government departments. As the result of such activities the work of government is given a degree of coherence.

3 Mobilising support for the policies of the government. This may involve liaising with members of the legislature or seeking to rally public opinion in support of government initiatives.

4 Acting in times of crisis when decisive action is required. Such firm leadership is usually best provided by a single person.

5 Appointing (and dismissing) other members of the executive branch.

There are broadly two models which describe the manner in which political power is allocated within the executive branch of government. Power may be held by the chief executive alone. This is the case in America where the president is regarded as the main source of power within the executive branch of government. He is separately elected and can thus claim an electoral mandate to initiate recommendations concerning public policy. Alternatively power may be held by a group of individuals who include the chief executive and other leading members of the government.

The term 'cabinet government' is used to describe this latter situation and is more likely to be found in parliamentary systems of government.

THE AMERICAN CABINET

The American Constitution made no reference to the concept of cabinet government. However, George Washington commenced the practice of holding regular meetings with senior members of his administration. Other Presidents followed suit, although cabinet government (in the sense of a group of equals meeting regularly and making collective decisions concerning policy) has never assumed the importance attached to it in other liberal democracies.

The cabinet is recognised in Germany's Basic Law and given a number of powers. These include the right to introduce legislation and the power to veto laws which increase expenditure or decrease income. In Britain there is a strong tradition of cabinet government. This suggests that political power is shared between the chief executive and other members of the government. Major issues of public policy are discussed by all members of the government as a team, presided over by the prime minister. In recent years, however, the nature of cabinet government in this country has been subject to debates which have questioned the ability of a small group of people to determine major issues of policy. It has been suggested that Britain's system of government has become 'prime ministerial' or 'presidential'. In the following section we examine these arguments in more detail.

Cabinet government in Britain

Why has it been alleged that the role of the cabinet has declined in modern government and how valid are these arguments?

The decline of cabinet government

For a number of years in Britain the extent to which the cabinet operates as the decision-making body at the very heart of government, exercising general superintendence over policy and providing cohesion to its affairs, has been questioned. The following arguments have been put forward to explain the decline of cabinet government.

Ministerial preoccupation with individual departments

It is argued that most members of the cabinet are preoccupied with the task of running their departments and thus lack the time or the inclination to involve themselves in affairs other than those with which they are directly concerned. Further, ministers in charge of departments may become parochial and seek to advance their department's interests which may be to the detriment of concern for overall planning.

Ministerial workloads

It has also been asserted that the extent of the work of contemporary government and its specialised nature means that decisions are made in forums other than at cabinet meetings (which are usually held weekly). These alternative arenas of policy making include cabinet committees which operate within the framework of the cabinet system. Alternatively decisions may be made using more informal structures which may be divorced from the structure of the cabinet. These include liaison between ministers or informal groupings centred on the prime minister which may comprise ministers and other advisers. It is thus asserted that the role of the cabinet is merely that of rubber-stamping decisions which have been reached elsewhere.

CABINET COMMITTEES

These enable ministers or civil servants to examine issues in depth, perhaps reporting the conclusions of their deliberations to the full cabinet. There are two types of such committees, permanent and *ad hoc*, which are serviced by the cabinet secretariat. In July 1995 it was revealed that there were 18 of these bodies. Key committees are chaired either by the prime minister or the deputy prime minister.

Prime ministerial government

It is also argued that modern prime ministers dominate the proceedings of their governments. General elections tend to place considerable prominence on the party leader thus enhancing the status of that person should he or she become prime minister. The prime minister possesses the power to appoint and dismiss other members of the government and manages the workings of the cabinet through the control of the agenda and summing up its proceedings. The development of a prime ministerial office has further increased the power of this official by providing a bureaucracy which gives advice on major issues of policy. This ensures that the prime minister possesses much information on the key affairs of state. It is thus argued that Britain's government has become prime ministerial or even presidential in nature.

The continued vitality of cabinet government

The argument that cabinet government has declined in Britain is not universally accepted. It is argued that the style or character of individual prime ministers has a bearing on the extent to which they wish to exercise initiative or resort to the teamwork of cabinet government to decide major policy issues. Further, prime ministers need to be wary of conduct which is viewed as overbearing by their cabinet colleagues. Resignations can have significant consequences for the prime minister's hold on office. Sir Geoffrey Howe's resignation from prime minister Thatcher's government in November 1990 had a major impact on the vitality of her administration.

It is also alleged that although the function of the cabinet has changed, it retains important roles in the affairs of modern government. It provides a mechanism for leading members of the government to be made aware of key political issues and provides the semblance of a unified government involved in collective decision making. The cabinet may also act as a final court of appeal to arbitrate disputes between ministers.

Chief executives and heads of state

What is a head of state, and what does this official do?

There is considerable variety within liberal democracies concerning the office of head of state. In countries such as Britain the head of state is a constitutional monarch, whose position is derived from birth. In other countries the head of state is elected. This may be direct election (as is the case in Ireland) or indirect election (as is the case in Italy where the president is elected by a college of 'grand electors' which includes members of both houses of parliament and regional governments). In most liberal democracies, the office of head of state is separate from that of chief executive, although in America the president occupies both roles.

A head of state performs important roles in the functioning of a liberal democracy. This official stands above party politics and constitutes the physical embodiment of the nation. This enables the head of state to provide a rallying point for national unity which may be especially important in times of crisis. Additionally, the head of state ensures that the system of government operates smoothly and efficiently. Many of the functions traditionally performed by a head of state are not controversial. These include receiving ambassadors from abroad or presiding over a range of official or ceremonial functions.

Typically heads of state appoint chief executives or signify the formal approval of legislation. In most cases these are endorsements of decisions which have already been made. But the participation of the head of state to some extent neutralises the party political dimension of the activity. The involvement of a head of state in selecting a chief executive, for example, seeks to suggest that this official serves the whole nation rather than the political interests which were responsible for securing the office for that person. A head of state usually possesses the ability to intervene in the conduct of political affairs. This intervention may seek to get a particularly contentious issue further examined, or the head of state may possess certain reserve powers (such as the ability to dismiss the government or dissolve the legislature) which serve to make the executive branch accountable to a higher authority for its actions. These powers are particularly important when there is an impasse in government.

One danger with a separately elected head of state is that this official may seek to use the authority derived from the position of an apolitical national leader to promote major governmental reform. This accusation was levelled against the Italian president, Francesco Corsiga (1985–92), who unsuccessfully sought to introduce a presidential regime coupled with the use of referendums to remedy what he viewed as the problems associated with parliamentary government.

The British monarchy
The British monarch is head of state and also head of the Commonwealth. Criticisms have been directed at the monarchy in Britain but also within the Commonwealth, most notably in Australia.

AUSTRALIA AND THE MONARCHY

The Australian Republican Movement was founded in 1991 to seek an Australian Republic by the year 2001 (the centenary of federation) in which an Australian citizen would be head of state. In 1993 the then prime minister, Paul Keating, appointed a Republic Advisory Committee to prepare options for public discussion and in 1995 announced that a referendum would be held on this subject. Mr Keating's defeat in the 1996 general election may serve to take this issue off the political agenda as the new prime minister, John Howard, does not have republican sympathies.

Critics argue that the monarchy instils society with values which are inappropriate for a liberal democracy. It transforms 'citizens' into 'subjects' and in particular suggests that birth rather than merit is a key determinant of a person's social position. The monarchy has also been condemned on grounds of cost. This has been compared unfavourably with other European constitutional monarchies, for example in Spain or the 'bicycling monarchies' found in Scandinavia. The key issue concerns the costs of the Court. In response to such criticisms it was announced in November 1992 that the Queen would pay tax on her personal income and would assume responsibility for the payments made from the Civil List to most members of the Royal Family. But although the Civil List voted by Parliament is a declining source of royal finance, public money is provided from other sources including government departments.

Further criticisms have been levelled against the monarchy for the role it performs in contemporary government. On the one hand it is alleged that many actions performed by the monarch are ceremonial (such as the state opening of Parliament) or are performed at the behest of others (such as granting Royal Pardons, which are determined by the Home Secretary). On the other hand fears are sometimes voiced concerning the monarch's intervention (or potential involvement) in political affairs. The monarch's choice of prime minister in Britain is normally confined to the leader of the largest party following a general election. However, if third parties assume a more dominant role in future years, the monarch may be required to intervene more frequently in the conduct of political affairs as has been the case in Belgium and the Netherlands. This involvement may extend to decisions relating to the dissolution of Parliament or the dismissal of a prime minister. Although no British prime minister has been dismissed by the monarch recently, the Australian prime minister, Gough Whitlam, was sacked in 1975 by the Queen's representative, the Governor-General.

THE ROYAL PREROGATIVE

The existence of the monarchy justifies the continuance of the royal prerogative. This gives the British government the ability to act in a number of matters without having to consult with Parliament. Declarations of war or the occasional use of troops in strikes are examples of actions undertaken by governments based on the use of the royal prerogative.

Although there have been reforms designed to introduce an element of accountability into the use of the royal prerogative (such as making the work of the intelligence services accountable to Parliament) it is argued by some that it is essentially inconsistent with the operations of a liberal democratic political system.

Such considerations have led to demands for a head of state who is politically accountable for his or her actions. Opinion polls, however, suggest that the monarchy continues to enjoy a relatively high level of public approval. Supporters will claim that much of the ceremony attached to the institution aids the tourist industry while royal tours abroad help exports. The non-partisan nature of the monarchy may also be depicted as a source of strength enabling governments to receive impartial advice from a seasoned political observer and giving the nation a symbol to rally around. This may be important in times of national emergency such as war or on occasions of national rejoicing such as the VE and VJ celebrations held in 1995.

The power of chief executives

What factors govern the ability of chief executives to achieve their political objectives?

It is often assumed that chief executives occupy a dominant position in the political system from which they are able to successfully advance initiatives designed to achieve their objectives or those of the government which they head. In this section we consider the difficulties which chief executives in Britain and America may encounter when seeking to advance their political aims and which thus serve as constraints on their power.

The British prime minister

It is frequently asserted that the prime minister possesses considerable control over the conduct of British political affairs. However, while there are few formal restraints on this office, the prime minister is subject to a range of informal pressures which may greatly limit that person's power.

Control of parliament

First the parliamentary situation may restrict the ability of a prime minister to achieve political objectives. The prime minister is the leader of the majority party in Parliament which means that the chief executive's ability to exercise control over political affairs is potentially greatest when that party has a sizeable majority in the House of Commons. A government with a small, or no, majority may have to rely on members drawn from other parties to sustain it in the regular votes which occur. In this circumstance the prime minister may have to agree to demands made by other politicians on whom the government is forced to rely.

Unity of the parliamentary party

A prime minister's power may also be affected by the unity of his or her parliamentary party. Internal divisions may exercise considerable influence on the composition of the government and a prime minister may be constrained to ensure that party balance is reflected in its make up. A disunited parliamentary party may make it difficult for the prime minister to secure the passage of policies through the House of Commons. Discontented members may abstain, vote against their own party or even defect to the opposition. This may increase the government's reliance on other parties to secure parliamentary victory. While a prime minister may threaten to quell revolts by the threat of dissolving parliament and holding a general election, this is a double-edged sword and is rarely a credible sanction which can be deployed.

CONSERVATIVE DISUNITY

The Conservative government was weakened by internal dissension during 1995, primarily associated with European policy. In December 1995 the government lost a key vote on fishing policy due to Eurosceptic hostility towards the European Union's common fishing policy.

Public opinion

Public opinion may also affect the power of the prime minister. Prime ministers may find it easiest to assert themselves when there is a demonstrable degree of support from the electorate for themselves and the governments which they head. When the level of this support declines (tested in opinion polls, parliamentary by-elections or local government elections) a prime minister is in a weaker position. Accordingly the ability to manipulate the media is of crucial importance to a contemporary prime minister. Margaret Thatcher's press secretary, Bernard Ingham, performed a major role between 1979 and 1990 in bolstering the power of the prime minister.

The loss of public support may not necessarily affect the conduct of the prime minister. This to a large extent depends on that person's nerve as to whether to ignore the loss of support and continue with existing policies or whether to bow to public pressure and make changes in either the personnel or the policy of the government.

CABINET RESHUFFLES

Cabinet re-shuffles have been traditionally used by prime ministers in many liberal democracies to increase the level of public support for themselves and the governments which they head. In September 1995 the French prime minister, Alain Juppé, dismissed 13 ministers in an attempt to reverse the decline in popularity experienced by his government.

The American president

The American Constitution placed the executive branch in the hands of a president who is directly elected. The president serves a term of four years and may be re-elected on one further occasion. The power exercised by a president to some extent depends on personal choice. Presidents may view themselves as an official who should merely enforce the laws passed by Congress or they may see themselves as a dynamic initiator of public policy. These views are further flavoured by popular opinion.

The belief that American presidents should be strong and assertive in the conduct of public affairs was bolstered by the need for decisive presidential action to cope with the Depression in the 1930s. But this view has subsequently been revised by the perceived failings of strong presidents as revealed by the outcome of the Vietnam War (which was associated with presidential initiative) and the belief that strong executive action can lead to abuse of power as was evidenced in Watergate and the subsequent forced resignation of President Nixon in 1974. Such factors have tended to make the public suspicious of presidents who wish to exercise dynamic leadership. Their ability to initiate actions has further been weakened by the size of the budget deficit which grew enormously during the Reagan–Bush years (1981–92) and served as a constraint on presidents who might wish to promote policies involving state intervention.

Such considerations have greatly affected the climate within which contemporary presidents operate. But within such a climate, presidents retain a considerable degree of manoeuvre. They possess a range of formal and informal powers and may also exploit their position as the only national unifying force to secure the attainment of their objectives. We shall now consider a range of factors which may have a bearing on the power of a modern president.

The president's mandate
The mandate which a president obtains in an election may greatly influence subsequent behaviour. A president may feel it is legitimate to exercise the initiative in public affairs when the outcome of an election provides a clear statement of public support for a stated programme. When the outcome of an election is less clear (for example, the president fails to secure a majority of the popular vote) or it appears that the result was more concerned with the rejection of one candidate than with the popular endorsement of the winner, the president may find it more difficult to vigorously promote policy especially when this involves initiating radical changes. Both of these factors played a part in influencing the effectiveness of President Clinton

following the 1992 election. Mr Clinton scored only 43.3% of the popular vote in an election which was widely seen as a vote against President Bush. At the same time, the Democratic party lost nine seats in the House of Representatives.

Clearly focused policy goals

Presidential success in initiating public policy may be most easily realised when policy goals are clearly focused. This suggests a limited set of key objectives which enable both Congress and public opinion in general to appreciate what are the president's fundamental concerns. It has been argued that President Carter (1977–81) put forward too disparate a range of proposals at the outset of his presidency which presented a confusing statement of presidential objectives. Accordingly President Reagan (1981–89) presented a programme which included fewer key issues. Subsequently relations with Congress were fashioned around achieving these. President Clinton's initial effort to focus on domestic policy issues was impeded by the emergence of defence and foreign policy issues (including the Bosnian crisis) which demanded attention at the expense of the original objectives.

Relations with congress

A president's relations with Congress have a fundamental bearing on that official's power. The president (unlike the British prime minister) has no direct connection with the legislature, and Congress may not be inclined to follow the presidential lead. Congress has become more assertive since the 1970s which has been to the detriment of presidents seeking to exercise a dominant role in both domestic and foreign affairs.

In domestic affairs, legislation such as the 1974 Budget and Impoundment Control Act introduced innovations designed to enable Congress to compete with the president in the preparation of the budget. In foreign affairs (which had been traditionally dominated by the president) legislation such as the 1973 War Powers Act and the 1976 National Emergencies Act limited the scope of presidential initiative. Congress's control over appropriations was used to stop aid to the Nicaraguan rebels in 1987. The end of the 'cold war' has further influenced Congressional involvement in foreign affairs. A major example was the vote of both houses of Congress in 1995 to overrule the president's policy of an embargo on the sale of arms to Bosnia.

Theoretically the party system might secure a degree of support for the president from within Congress but this does not operate in the same way as it does in Britain. Changes to the process by which presidential candidates are nominated and the manner in which presidential election campaigns are financed has been to the detriment of the relationship between a president and established party organisation. Further, parochialism exerts considerable influence over the conduct of members of Congress. Thus they may be more willing to follow the president's lead when they feel this will bring personal political benefits to them but be inclined to distance themselves from the administration if they feel that association with the president constitutes an electoral liability.

Thus even when the president's party controls both Houses of Congress, this is no guarantee that all members of that party will support the president on every major policy initiative. President Carter, for example, did not construct good working relationships with his own party which controlled both Houses of Congress throughout his presidency. However, the position of the president is weaker when the opposition party controls either or both houses of Congress. This is a position of 'gridlock' which post-war Republican presidents frequently had to endure but which was inflicted on President Clinton following the loss of Democrat majorities in both Houses at the November 1994 Congressional elections.

'DIVIDED GOVERNMENT' IN AMERICA

In a situation of 'divided government' there is no onus on the Congressional majority to aid the passage of the president's programme and their own leadership might attempt to seize the initiative in policy making. After November 1994 the Republican Speaker of the House of Representatives, Newt Gingrich, and the Republican majority leader in the Senate, Robert Dole, exercised a role in policy initiation which seemed to eclipse that exerted by President Clinton.

In such situations presidents may seek to bargain with Congress in order to retain some influence over the legislative process. If Congress puts forward legislative proposals, the president is able to veto them. Although Congress may be able to override this veto, the threat or actuality of using it may trigger off a process of bargaining between the president and congressional opposition.

However, the result may be that neither side will give way to the other. The inability of president and Congress to resolve disagreements on the budget in 1995 led to a shutdown in government in which federal employees were sent home when conditions attached by Congress for the approval of government expenditure were rejected by the president.

Conclusion – how presidents may achieve their goals
Contemporary presidents may seek to overcome the difficulties which impede the attainment of their goals in a number of ways. In situations of 'divided' and 'unified' government a president is required to build coalitions within Congress to secure the passage of key legislation. It is a process which has been complicated by Congressional reforms initiated after Watergate, especially in connection with the committee system, which have tended to disperse power within Congress. This has made it harder for a president to manage this body through relationships forged with a relatively small number of senior, influential members of Congress.

This process of coalition building often involves securing support from politicians of different political allegiances by lobbying, persuading or even coercing them to support the president. It may require coalitions to be constructed on an issue-by-issue basis and has become a key feature of what has been termed the 'no win' presidency. Presidents such as Lyndon Johnson who learned their trade on the 'Hill' were able to conduct this 'wheeling and dealing' successfully especially in connection with his 'Great Society' programme. Others whose political experience was different (such as President Carter who was elected as an 'outsider' to Washington politics) were less successful coalition builders and found problems in persuading Congress to implement their programmes.

Relations with the media may also influence a president's power. A popular president is likely to find it easier to secure support within Congress for the administration's policies and traditionally presidents went to great lengths to ensure that they received favourable treatment by the media. However, in the post-Watergate period the media has become prone to subjecting the president to critical analysis. There are ways to counter this, in particular by seeking to ensure that the president's message is not mediated by the media but is heard (or received) directly by the people. This technique was particularly developed by President F.D. Roosevelt whose 'fireside chats' enabled him to address his message directly into the homes of the American public. Such tactics may enable a president to circumvent obstacles which threaten to impede the progress of key policies. Nonetheless, the ability of the media to subject the president to critical analysis is an important force which may weaken the president in the eyes of the population.

THE AMERICAN VICE-PRESIDENCY

The American constitution provided for a vice-president who would take over on the 'death, resignation or inability' of the president. The circumstances under which this official would assume the office of president was subsequently expanded upon in the twenty-fifth amendment, passed in 1967. Otherwise the vice-president's main function was to act as president of the senate with the power to vote when there was a tie.

Traditionally the office has not been highly regarded. When Lyndon Johnson considered Kennedy's offer of the vice-presidency in 1960, he contacted John Garner who had occupied this post under President Roosevelt from 1933–41. Garner reputedly informed Johnson that the office was not worth 'a pitcher of warm spit'. However some recent presidents have given their vice-presidents a more significant role. President Carter (1977–81) made prominent use of Walter Mondale. This included involvement in the operations of the White House.

Service as vice-president is no guarantee of becoming president when the incumbent retires. George Bush in 1988 was the first serving vice-president to be elected president since Martin Van Buren in 1836.

The chief executive's bureaucracy

What machinery exists to enable a chief executive to dominate the executive branch of government?

The scope of contemporary government requires those exercising control over it to possess detailed knowledge of complex and technical policy areas. Bureaucracies have thus been developed to serve the chief executive, enabling him or her to exert overall control within the executive branch of government. Such bureaucracies fulfill a number of functions. These include the provision of advice on policy matters. This gives the chief executive expertise which may provide leverage in dealings with the civil service employed elsewhere within the executive branch. Their role also includes performing functions designed to secure the success of policy initiatives put forward by the chief executive and may actually implement policy in certain areas.

Examples of bureaucracies serving chief executives

In America President F.D. Roosevelt established the Executive Office of the President in 1939. This contains three bodies – the National Security Council, the Council of Economic Advisers and the Office of Management and Budget. Their work is supplemented by the White House staff which includes the key aides seen on a regular basis by the president.

The German chancellor has a personal department, the *Bundeskanzleramt*. This body is chiefly responsible for coordinating, planning and implementing policy and also ensures that the chancellor's policies are disseminated throughout the party and to the general public.

The French president has a presidential office, the General Secretariat of the Presidency, which includes a number of advisors. There is also the *cabinet du president* which contains personal presidential aides.

The British prime minister has the Prime Minister's Office. This contains a policy unit (sometimes referred to as the 'Number 10 Policy Unit') which gives advice, monitors and develops policy. The Prime Minister's office gives the prime minister detailed knowledge of the affairs of government and enhances his or her ability to initiate policies.

Problems associated with chief executives' bureaucracies

While such bureaucracies give chief executives a greater ability to assert control over governments, we should note that there are problems associated with the role which these bodies perform. One major difficulty with such machinery is its size. As the number of staff which are employed within such bodies grows, it becomes increasingly difficult for the chief executive to maintain control over its work. This was a major problem for President Reagan whose personal reputation suffered in the 'Iran–Contra' affair. The president was held responsible for the actions of others which were undertaken in his name. A further danger is that such bureaucracies may insulate the chief executive from outside pressures to such an extent that they lose touch with the 'real world'. This may damage their chances of re-election to office.

A final difficulty is that the role performed by the chief executive's advisers may eclipse that of departments headed by leading members of the government. President Nixon's national security adviser in his first term, Dr Henry Kissinger, had a national and international profile which surpassed that of the Secretary of State. Leading politicians may resent being effectively sidelined by an entourage of unelected advisers and this friction may have damaging repercussions for the stability of the government. In 1989 the British Chancellor of the Exchequer, Nigel Lawson, resigned because of the influence exerted by Prime Minister Thatcher's adviser on economic affairs, Sir Alan Walters.

Questions

1 List what you consider to be the essential differences between a parliamentary and a presidential system of government.
2 Consider the advantages of:
   (a) A constitutional monarch
        and
   (b) An elected president
        performing the functions of head of state.
3 What are the key features of cabinet government? What factors hinder its operations in contemporary liberal democracies with a tradition of this method of government?
4 Based on the accounts of the British prime minister and the American president provided in this chapter, what do you consider to be the main factors which limit the ability of modern chief executives to secure their political goals? How might these limitations be overcome?

Summary

1 In liberal democratic political systems political control over a
nation's affairs is entrusted to a small group of politicians. These
perform the executive tasks of government. Such executives may
be parliamentary or presidential. In the former system the
executive is drawn from the legislature and is accountable to it
while in the latter the executive is directly elected. France possesses
a hybrid system, the essential feature of which is the changing
balance of power between the president and prime minister.

2 Leadership within the executive branch of government is provided
by a chief executive whose role includes overseeing the
administration and execution of policy and acting in time of crisis.
A chief executive may be dominant in the executive branch of
government (as is the case in America) or control over the conduct
of political affairs may be shared with other members of that
branch. Britain is an example of a country in which the latter
situation prevails and a tradition of cabinet government exists,
although its role has changed in recent years.

3 Many liberal democracies possess a head of state who stands above
party politics and acts as the physical embodiment of national
unity. A head of state may be elected (as in Ireland) or be an
hereditary monarch (which is the case in Britain and the
Commonwealth countries). In America the president combines the
office of chief executive with that of head of state.

4 The power of chief executives is not absolute. In both parliamentary
and presidential systems of government an array of formal and
informal factors restrict the ability of these officials to achieve
their political goals. The British prime minister may be constrained
by the political composition of the legislature, the unity of his or
her political party and public opinion. An American president is
restricted by factors which include the aftermath of Watergate, the
size of the budget deficit and problems in exercising control over
Congress. It may be further impeded by a situation of 'gridlock' in
which Congress is controlled by the party in opposition to the
president. Coalition building or the skilful use of the media may
help to restore some aspects of presidential initiative.

5 The power of contemporary chief executives is enhanced by the
development of bureaucracies (such as the Executive Office of the

American President) which serve such officials. But problems have been associated with the role performed by such bodies, especially when they effectively sideline other leading members of the executive branch of government.

9
THE BUREAUCRACY

Role

Who are bureaucrats, and what role do they perform in contemporary government?

This aspect of our study concerns the administrative arm of the executive branch of government. Here the work is performed by paid officials whom we term 'bureaucrats'. Many of these are categorised as civil servants. This means that key matters such as recruitment, pay, promotion, grading, dismissal and conditions of work are subject to common regulations which operate throughout the national government within which they work. Such common regulations are enforced centrally by bodies such as the American Office of Personnel Management or the British Civil Service Commission

Civil servants perform a variety of roles in liberal democratic states, but there are two which have traditionally been emphasised. They give advice to those who exercise control of the political arm of the executive branch on the content of policy. They may also be responsible for implementing it.

POLICY IMPLEMENTATION

The implementation of policy is carried out at all levels of government and includes the delivery of a service to the public (such as the payment of welfare benefits). Policy implementation by the civil service is typically characterised by the impersonal application of established rules and procedures. We sometimes use the term 'red tape' to describe the consequences of this method of operation.

The development of the bureaucracy differs from one country to an other. Initially jobs in government service were often allocated through the patronage system. Thus people were employed on the basis of personal or family contacts rather than their ability to perform efficiently the tasks which their job involved. This system, in which political loyalty was more important than personal competence, tended to promote inefficiency in the operations of the public sector. It was a problem which many countries addressed during the nineteenth century. Below we briefly examine the experience of two countries – Britain and America.

Civil service reform in Britain

In Britain the major impetus to the reform of the nineteenth century civil service was provided by a commission which included Sir Stafford Northcote and Sir Charles Trevelyan. This reported in 1854 and recommended that a distinction should be drawn between routine work and that which required intellectual ability. It was suggested that the latter should be carried out by appointees who were chosen on the basis of their performance in an examination of a literary kind, based on subjects studied at the universities. In 1855 three civil service commissioners were appointed to conduct such examinations, which in 1870 were made open to all suitably qualified members of the general public.

This report gave the British civil service certain key characteristics. These were the generalist tradition of the higher civil service (in which the ability to implement decisions was given a higher priority than expertise in policy areas), permanence (which viewed the job as a career performed by servants of the Crown rather than a temporary position dependent on political patronage), neutrality (which derived from the permanence principle and suggested that a civil servant could serve any government impartially, regardless of its politician complexion), and anonymity (whereby ministers were publicly accountable for the actions undertaken by the government departments, and civil servants traditionally remained silent on issues affecting public policy). The generalist tradition also facilitated movement of civil servants between government departments, thus fostering the concept of a unified civil service.

Civil service reform in America

Political patronage also influenced the appointment, promotion and dismissal of those employed in American federal public service for much of the nineteenth century. President Andrew Jackson played a key role in developing the 'spoils system' when he assumed office in 1829. This viewed public office as a legitimate prize with which politicians could reward their supporters. Only towards the end of that century did pressure exerted by bodies such as the National Civil Service Reform League succeed in promoting change. In 1883 the Pendleton Act established the Civil Service Commission (later renamed the Office of Personnel Management). This was a bipartisan board of three members which was charged with setting examinations which a candidate had to pass as a condition of appointment into certain civil service jobs. Initially a relatively limited number of posts were affected by this reform, but the number extended during the twentieth century. Today the bulk of civil service posts are covered by 'civil service rules' operated by the Office of Personnel Management. The main criterion for obtaining a job is merit displayed in a competitive examination.

A further characteristic of the American civil service is political neutrality. Under the provisions of the 1939 and 1940 Hatch Acts, civil servants are forbidden to take any active part in political management or political campaigns. However, this situation is offset by the situation that a considerable number of posts in the federal government's civil service remain at the disposal of a president. An incoming president retains the ability to appoint a number of key personnel in the federal government, although the most senior (at deputy secretary, under secretary and assistant secretary levels) are subject to Senate confirmation. These total about 600 posts. The president's appointing power for a further group of senior executive service posts (about 700 in number) is constrained by the 1978 Civil Service Reform Act.

The machinery of government

How is the machinery of government organised?

The existence of government departments is sometimes determined by legislation. In Ireland, for example, the 1924 Ministers and

Secretaries Act provided the legal basis for the establishment of the Departments of State and the allocation of work between them. Chief executives may possess the ability to initiate reorganisation to the structure of government by abolishing existing departments, creating new ones or reallocating the tasks of government between departments. However, political constraints frequently restrict the scope of such changes. This tends to mean that changes made by a chief executive to the structure of government are often of an incremental nature, marginally adjusting, but not radically overhauling, the organisation which existed when the chief executive assumed office. We examine this proposition by considering the case of Britain.

THE DEPLOYMENT OF CIVIL SERVANTS

The civil service is a hierarchical organisation which utilises common structures such as grades and classes to establish a chain of command and to differentiate work according to the complexity of the tasks involved. A key distinction exists between those who perform routine administrative or clerical duties and the higher civil service who liaise with ministers and are the managers of government departments.

Civil servants working for national governments are based in a variety of bodies. Many are employed in government departments or in agencies which have a formal reporting relationship with such bodies. Political control over departments and their related organisations is exercised by a person appointed by the chief executive. This person is frequently termed a 'minister' or (in America) a 'secretary'.

The organisation of the British machinery of government

In this section we consider the organisation of British central government. We are using Britain as a case study to examine the principles which have been applied by successive prime ministers to provide for the allocation of the work of government between departments.

Non-rational considerations such as a prime minister's desire to emphasise commitment to a particular policy area, the need to ensure that major responsibilities are evenly distributed between senior political colleagues and the preferences of pressure groups play an important part in determining the way in which government departments are organised. Such political pressures may promote change or prevent it from occurring. Nonetheless, attempts have been made to organise the British machinery of government in a logical manner.

The expanded role of the state during the First World War prompted the prime minister, David Lloyd George, to appoint a Machinery of Government committee, headed by Lord Haldane, to consider the organisation of government departments. This committee reported in 1919. Lord Haldane considered two alternative methods – organising departments around a specific category of citizen whose needs were handled by a department (which was termed the 'client principle') or according to a particular service delivered by a department. His report recommended the latter method of organisation which tended to justify the existence of departments whose range of policy was relatively narrow.

The increase of state functions during and after the Second World War thus resulted in the creation of a large number of separate government departments. As the ministers which headed them could not all be included in a prime minister's cabinet (since to do so would have created a body too large for decision making), this body's role as the co-ordinator of the entire work of government was placed in jeopardy. Various expedients were put forward in an attempt to remedy this problem. Prime Minister Churchill introduced the 'overlord system' in 1951 which involved the appointment of three co-ordinating ministers to represent at cabinet level the interests of a number of departments which retained their independent status. The blurred nature of responsibility between the departmental minister and the overlord led to the abandonment of this system in 1953. It was followed in the 1960s by physically merging departments whose responsibilities were related. In 1964 the Ministry of Defence was established, followed by the Foreign and Commonwealth Office and the Department of Health and Social Security in 1968. The term 'giant department' described the expanded policy areas controlled by these bodies.

The advantage possessed by giant departments was that they enabled a prime minister to ensure that all major areas of government activity were represented at cabinet level. However, the size of these departments (measured in terms of the staff they employed and the range of policy embraced within them) raised doubts as to whether effective managerial or political control could be exerted over them.

In 1970 the newly-elected Conservative government produced a white paper, entitled 'The Reorganisation of Central Government'. This proposed organising the machinery of government according to what was termed the 'functional principle'. This principle was summarised by the assertion that 'organisation should be the servant of policy' and implied that the machinery of government should be structured according to specific objectives which ministers wished to achieve. Its main benefit was stated to be the planning and implementation of a programme which would be in one set of hands rather than being shared between a number of departments with the inevitable problems of co-ordination and communication.

In practice, however, the white paper did not initiate any major departure in the manner in which government departments were organised. The two new organisations which were established (the Department of the Environment and the Department of Trade and Industry) were essentially giant departments in the mould of those created during the 1960s.

Subsequently changes have been made to departmental organisation with the creation of new departments (such as National Heritage), the division or abolition of existing departments and the reallocation of functions between them. A major change was the abolition of the Department of Employment in 1995 and the reallocation of its main functions between the Department of Trade and Industry and the re-named Department of Education and Employment. But these alterations have not been based on any attempt to recast the structure of government according to any rational principle or formula.

Civil service influence over policy making

Does the influence possessed by civil servants over the content of public policy go beyond the provision of advice to politicians?

This question compels us to consider whether the theoretical division between politics and administration is a meaningful one. In theory, senior civil servants give advice to politicians but it is the latter who take decisions. The role of the civil service then becomes that of implementing these decisions. The key issue concerns the extent to which the provision of advice by senior civil servants enables them to dominate the policy-making process. It is argued that the role of civil servants sometimes goes beyond the mere provision of advice and entails the exertion of a considerable degree of influence over the content of public policy. Civil servants act as both policy makers and policy implementors.

The accusation that civil servants usurped the role which ought to be fulfilled by politicians within the executive branch of government has been voiced in Britain in recent years. An extreme form of this argument has been that senior civil servants might conspire to prevent ministers from pursuing a course of action which they wished to embark upon. Below we examine this argument in greater detail.

Minister–civil servant relationship in Britain

The aim of this case study is to consider why and how civil servants might occupy a dominant position in policy making.

Civil servants are permanent officials with expertise (either of a policy area or of the workings of the administrative machine). Ministers hold office temporarily. They are 'here now and gone tomorrow'. Additionally, ministers may know little or nothing of the work of a department until they are placed in charge of it by a prime minister. Although they may employ a limited number of policy advisers, these are heavily outnumbered by permanent officials. In theory, therefore, civil servants are in a powerful position to overawe ministers but in any case many will be voluntarily disposed to defer to the views or wishes of their permanent officials. Some ministers will by choice take little part in policy making and be content to legitimise decisions made on their behalf by their civil servants.

The workload of a minister needs to be taken into account. A minister is also a Member of Parliament who needs to devote some time to constituency affairs. He or she is a leading member of a political party who is expected to perform activities to promote that party. A minister may additionally be a member of the cabinet and thus need to devote energy to the overall work of government. It would thus be physically impossible for a minister to supervise all aspects of a department's affairs. Thus ministers rely heavily on civil servants using their initiative to resolve unimportant or routine issues. These constitute the bulk of a department's work which does not, therefore, come before the minister for consideration. This gives the civil service the ability to make decisions over a very wide range of departmental activities in which the only political guideline might be that of 'knowing the minister's mind' – that is assessing how the minister would act if he or she were available to deal with the situation personally.

The above arguments suggest that ministers may acquiesce to a wide range of civil service policy making. Problems arise only when ministers perceive civil servants acting improperly by seeking to control the policy-making process by the manipulation or obstruction of ministers.

Many ministers make decisions by selecting from options presented to them by the civil service. This gives the civil service ample opportunity to guide the minister in the direction in which they wish him or her to go. They may do this, for example, by producing an incomplete list of options designed to direct the minister towards the course of action favoured by the department. Alternatively they may attempt to 'blind a minister with science' that is, make an issue seem so technical that the minister, as a layperson, feels uncomfortable and thus disposed towards accepting the preferred view of the civil service.

However, some ministers wish to exercise a more prominent role concerning policy making. They enter office with clearly defined policy objectives and an appreciation concerning how these goals should be accomplished. However, this does not guarantee that the civil service will follow the minister's lead. They may utilise an array of devices to stop, or slow down, the implementation of the minister's wishes. Such tactics include deliberately delaying the implementation of ministerial directives or mobilising opposition to the minister's policy. The latter may involve the use of machinery such as inter-departmental committees (which are staffed by senior civil servants and from which ministers are excluded) to mobilise opposition to a minister's policy from civil servants drawn from a number of departments. Alternatively civil servants might manufacture political pressure against a minister which is designed to secure the abandonment of the politician's preferred course of action. They may do this by appealing over the head of the minister to the prime minister or the cabinet, possibly utilising the argument that the minister's intended actions are contrary or damaging to overall government policy. The success of such a tactic is considerably influenced by the minister's standing among his or her political colleagues.

However, the argument that civil servants conspire to dominate the policy making process is not accepted as a universal truth. Although there may be occasions when this has happened, the relationship between ministers and their civil servants is frequently harmonious. Both need each other. The minister relies on the civil service for advice and the handling of routine business to ensure a manageable workload but the civil service rely on the minister to promote the department's interests. This may involve defending the department when its interests or activities are scrutinised by the cabinet or within Parliament. It may also involve performing an ambassadorial role to convince the general public that the department fulfils a vital role in civil affairs.

Political control

How can political control over the bureaucracy be secured?

There are various ways whereby the operations of the bureaucracy can be made susceptible to political influences. Ministers may appoint their own advisers to offset the activities of civil servants. One problem is that if these advisers are outsiders they may effectively be 'frozen out' of the operations of a department by its permanent officials. In France this difficulty is solved by ministers appointing existing civil servants to act as their advisers. These are located in the *cabinet ministériel*. They operate under the minister's direct control and usually revert to their previous posts when their service to the minister has ended.

Chief executives may also seek to exert influence over civil service actions. They may do this through involvement in the appointment, promotion and removal of civil servants. A major difficulty with such courses of action is that the civil service might become politicised. This means it becomes so closely identified with the policies of a particular political party that its neutrality (which is essential if it is to serve governments of other political persuasions) is questioned.

POLITICAL CONTROL OVER BRITISH CIVIL SERVICE APPOINTMENTS

Political involvement in appointments has been a particular issue in Britain during the 1980s when it has been alleged that the Conservative Party subjected the higher echelons of the civil service to a considerable degree of political pressure to conform to the policies or working practices of the government. This was summarised in the phrase 'one of us' which allegedly was a test applied by the government to the promotion of civil servants to the post of permanent and deputy secretary.

The legislature may also exert influence over the conduct of the bureaucracy. In Britain, for example, special investigations may be launched by bodies such as Parliamentary select committees into the operations of particular departments or agencies.

In assessing the effectiveness of political control over the bureaucracy, however, we must be aware of a potential conflict between accountability and managerial freedom. Although those whose activities are financed by public money need to account for what they do, excessive accountability tends to stifle initiative and make civil servants operate in a cautious manner dominated by adherence to stipulated procedures. Ideally, therefore, agencies should be accountable for their results but given a degree of discretion as to how these are achieved.

Below we examine the methods which are utilised in America to subject the bureaucracy to political influences.

Control of the American federal bureaucracy

In America the control of the federal bureaucracy involves both the president and Congress. Their involvement is sometimes prompted by a belief that inadequate control results in waste and inefficiency. The president may seek to exert control over the bureaucracy in a number of ways. Commissions may be appointed to scrutinise its workings. Additionally, the president may install a number of political appointees into the federal bureaucracy to advance policy initiatives and install advisers, especially within the White House staff. Executive orders may be issued to agencies. During the 1980s President Reagan further sought to use the Office of Management and Budget to ensure that agency regulations conformed to administration policy.

INVESTIGATIONS INTO THE FEDERAL BUREAUCRACY

In 1982 President Reagan's appointed a commission chaired by Peter Grace to find ways to reduce government spending and to eliminate bureaucratic waste and mismanagement. This commission reported that the government was the worst run enterprise in America.

There are, however, a number of problems which impede effective presidential control over the federal bureaucracy. These include its fragmented nature. It is composed of a variety of departments, agencies, bureaux and commissions which possess varying degrees of autonomy. Presidential control may also be hindered by the relationship which such bodies are able to establish with Congress. Congress is required to approve proposals put forward by the president to reorganise government departments. Its opposition prevented President Nixon from amalgamating seven departments into four 'super' departments in 1971 and halted President Reagan's plans to abolish the Departments of Education and Energy during the 1980s. Further, the 'iron triangle' relationships which may be constructed between agencies, congressional committees and clients or interest groups may also prove impenetrable to presidential control.

Congress, however, may have its own reasons for wishing to exert control over the operations of the federal bureaucracy. It may seek to ensure that its policy goals are fulfilled by the federal bureaucracy. Such is especially important in a situation of 'divided government' when Congress and the president may differ on the objectives which they wish the bureaucracy to achieve. There are a number of ways whereby Congress may seek to assert its control over the federal civil service. Control over funds is a key aspect of Congressional oversight which is asserted during the annual appropriations procedure. Some agencies or programmes are also subject to annual renewal which is based upon an assessment by Congress as to whether their aims are being accomplished. Bodies such as the General Accounting Office and the Office of Technology Assessment help to procure information to aid the oversight function. Congress may also launch special investigations into particular government activities. An example of this was the examination of the Central Intelligence Agency conducted during the 1970s.

CONGRESS AND BUREAUCRATIC PRACTICES

Congress has involved itself in the working practices of the bureaucracy. The exercise of discretion is governed by the 1946 Administrative Procedures Act and the 1990 Negotiated Rule Making Act.

The concern of Congress to secure efficiency and effectiveness within the civil service was displayed by the requirement in 1978 that all major agencies should appoint inspectors general, accountable to Congress (who were concerned with problems such as fraud and waste) and by the 1993 Government Performance and Results Act which introduced the practice of agencies (initially on a pilot basis) preparing annual development plans with measurable objectives to enable performance to be monitored.

Civil service influence throughout society

To what extent are civil servants a ruling elite?

The description of senior civil servants as an 'elite' particularly refers to their social background. In many countries such officials derive from a middle and upper middle class background. The stereotypical British senior civil servant is middle class, male, educated at public school and Oxford or Cambridge universities. A similar situation exists in France where, despite efforts by socialist administrations to broaden the recruitment base of such officials, a large number derive from socially exclusive backgrounds. There are, however, exceptions: in New Zealand, for example, the main source of recruitment into the civil service is from secondary school graduates. Preference is given to internal promotions to fill higher level vacancies.

Concern has been expressed that senior civil servants are able to imbue policy making with attitudes and values derived from their untypical social backgrounds. In some countries, however, the influence they possess extends throughout society and is not confined to the machinery of government. Let us consider the situation in France.

France: the administrators' state?

In France an elite group of persons trained as administrators occupy key positions in not only the civil service but also in political and commercial life in both the public and private sectors. Specialist training schools function as recruiting agencies for key areas of government activity. The most influential are the *Ecole Nationale d'Administration* and the *Ecole Polytechnique*. Their role is to recruit and train candidates for the higher level civil service posts. Such training involves education and practical experience. Successful graduates are able to secure posts in the most prestigious areas of government activity. Additionally, however, their background and training enable them to move from the public to the private sector and occupy senior positions there or to occupy key positions in other aspects of public affairs.

ADMINISTRATORS AND POLITICS

Bodies such as the *Ecole Nationale d'Administration* possess considerable prestige. The administrative court system is dominated by graduates from this institution.

The absence of any requirement that civil servants should not participate in political activities further increases the likelihood of administrators playing an active part in politics. The current president, Jacques Chirac, and his socialist opponent in the 1995 election, Lionel Jospin, were both graduates of the *Ecole Nationale d'Administration*.

Although the French administrative elite do not monopolise influential jobs throughout society, the dominant positions held by many from such a background has given rise to accusations that France is an 'administrator's state' in which persons trained as civil servants are dominant in all walks of life.

Reform of the civil service

Why has civil service reform been pursued vigorously in a number of countries in recent years and what direction has this reform taken?

The growth in the role of the state in a number of countries after 1945 resulted in a large civil service. This was costly. Thus governments wishing to prune public spending were induced to cast a critical eye at the workings of the bureaucracy. The reform of the civil service has been advocated in many countries. In Ireland the Devlin Report put forward reform proposals in 1969. In Britain the Fulton Report in 1968 and the Ibbs Report in 1988 influenced significant changes within the British civil service. In America this subject was recently considered by Vice-President Gore's *National Performance Review* published in 1993. Governments influenced by 'New Right' ideology have been especially interested in civil service reform in recent years. While it would be impossible to chart the directions which civil service reform has taken in various countries, there are certain developments which have occurred widely. We consider some of these common themes below.

Efficiency and value for money

The objective of effective management has commonly been implemented by drawing upon a number of management techniques utilised in the world of business by which efficiency can be monitored. These include the specification of departmental objectives and the preparation of performance indicators against which the attainment of objectives can be judged.

In Britain the concern for the elimination of waste and promotion of efficiency resulted in initiatives designed to establish accountable management within departments. This suggestion was made in the Fulton Report in 1968 and was pursued more vigorously following the 1979 general election when emphasis was placed on identifying the activities performed by units within a department in order for ministers to be more fully aware of that body's overall operations. Such an understanding paved the way for devolving managerial and budgetary responsibility to such units which could then more easily be held accountable by the minister for the performance of their duties.

During the 1980s scrutinies conducted by Lord Rayner's Efficiency Unit, the introduction of the Management Information System for Ministers (MINIS) into the Department of the Environment and the Financial Management Initiative were all concerned with the promotion of efficiency and value for money within central government.

The separation of policy planning and service delivery

A second direction which civil service reform has taken has been an attempt to redefine the role and organisation of national bureaucracies. Typically this involved the separation of policy planning from service delivery. There are two main advantages associated with this reform.

First, it gave key civil servants greater ability to engage in long-term planning by placing the day-to-day administration of services into the hands of bodies other than government departments. It has been argued that the British senior civil service's preoccupation with administration rather than planning resulted in a dislike of change and innovation. This reform would enhance the capacity of senior civil servants to plan. Second, those responsible for implementing services (usually in 'agencies') would exercise a considerable degree of discretion and operational freedom. This would improve the morale and motivation of the staff employed in such work. Within the confines of policy objectives and a budget set by a government department, those who delivered services would be delegated a wide degree of authority as to how they achieved their set goals.

Below we briefly consider the progress of this reform in Britain.

The 'Next Steps' Programme in Britain
In 1988 the Ibbs Report recommended that the national bureaucracy should be divided into a central civil service (which would advise ministers and be responsible for strategic planning within a department) and agencies (which would deliver the services within the framework devised by the department's central civil service). The rationale of this reform was to secure efficiency by freeing service delivery from what was perceived as the stultifying influence of traditional civil service working practices. Those who performed services were to be given a wide degree of discretion as to how they secured the objectives which were allotted to them. This recommendation was adopted by the government and became known as the 'Next Steps' Programme. The executive functions of central government would be performed by agencies, headed by a chief executive and staffed by civil servants.

Before an agency is set up ministers have to agree that the activity needs to be discharged by government. The alternatives of contracting out or privatisation have first to be considered. The relationships between departments and agencies are defined in a framework agreement. Innovations which were introduced included flexibility in recruitment, the development of pay and grading structures specific to agencies and the requirement that such bodies produce business plans and performance targets. Agency chief executives are appointed on fixed-term contracts and are paid bonuses to meet targets.

Agencies now dominate the central machinery of government. Over 60 per cent of all civil servants are employed by such bodies.

A number of criticisms have been made of the operation of agencies. It has been argued that they are insufficiently accountable for their actions. The convention of individual ministerial responsibility is harder to enforce when a wide range of operational decisions are made by civil servants who operate at arm's length from effective ministerial control. Further, such reforms tend to undermine the tradition of a unified civil service. The essence of this principle is that civil servants are able to move across departments and work anywhere within the bureaucracy. Such movement is less likely as the innovations referred to above tend to promote the view that workers are agency rather than government employees.

AGENCIES AND ACCOUNTABILITY

Ministers may use the existence of agencies to deny personal liability for the actions undertaken by civil servants.

In October 1995, for example, the Home Secretary denied responsibility for day-to-day operational activities in the prison service. These were stated to be the concern of Derek Lewis, who had occupied the position of Director General of the Prison Service. Issues related to prison security were thus declared to be an agency matter for which ministers could not be held to account.

Privatisation

A third direction which reform affecting the civil service frequently takes is for services to be delivered by private sector organisations. This is commonly referred to as privatisation. These services may be contracted out (in which case the civil service is involved in drawing up contracts which are subject to competitive tendering and then in monitoring the performance of those to whom such contracts are awarded) or they may be divorced from government completely. Such reforms view competition as the main way to make services become responsive to public demand.

Contracting out was pursued in America during the 1980s and the *National Performance Review* (1993) urged that increased use should be made of service provision by non-governmental bodies. During the 1990s, 'market testing' was introduced by the British government. This sought to establish the advantages of government departments contracting out a range of services to the private sector.

THE PROGRESS OF CIVIL SERVICE REFORMS

There may be problems when public policy is discharged by the private sector. Contracting out illustrates some of the difficulties which are involved. A full evaluation first needs to be undertaken to ascertain if it is appropriate for a service to be delivered by the private sector. If a service is contracted out it is essential that efficient monitoring procedures are put in place by departments to ensure that services are efficiently provided and to safeguard the interests of consumers. Such mechanisms involve cost but may also create tensions by seeking to evaluate the performance of those involved in commercial activities according to civil service standards.

Civil service inertia also needs to be overcome. Bureaucracies are often resistant to change, especially when organisations and jobs are threatened. Thus political will to implement reforms is important. The commitment of the Conservative government in Britain during the 1980s was crucial to bringing about alterations to the British civil service.

Criticisms have been directed against the involvement of the private sector in administering public policy. It is alleged that the private sector's main concern is profitability. The organisations which administer privatised services are said to be primarily motivated by a desire to make profits rather than to deliver a service to the public. In Britain, the government's response to such arguments has been to place emphasis on consumerism. The *Citizens' Charter* (1991) sought to make all providers of public services (including those administered by the private sector) aware of their duties to their clients and to establish standards of service which consumers had the right to expect.

Official secrecy

To what extent are the operations of central government subject to effective public scrutiny?

In a liberal democracy members of the general public need to be in a position to evaluate the performance of a government in order to give or deny that government political support. However, the secrecy which often surrounds the workings of government may make it difficult for the public to evaluate its operations. To do so requires the provision of information by which public policy can be judged.

FREEDOM OF INFORMATION LEGISLATION

Freedom of information legislation typically compels public bodies or officials to make available a wide range of material relevant to political affairs provided that this does not threaten national security or constitute an unwarranted intrusion into an individual's privacy. This legislation exists in America and Germany and is a considerable aid to investigative journalism.

In countries such as Britain and Ireland the media might find its ability to discuss political issues hampered. Here the absence of such legislation is coupled with the presence of laws limiting disclosure of information on the grounds of official secrecy.

In America the 1966 and 1974 Freedom of Information Acts provided citizens and interest groups with the right to inspect most federal records. Although access to some information may be denied, an appeal to the courts may secure the production of the desired material. New Zealand also has an Official Information Act which permits public access to a wide range of information.

In Britain there is no such legislation. Indeed, the 1911 Official Secrets Act made any disclosure of official information a criminal offence. This posed dilemmas for some civil servants. They sometimes believed that politicians confused state interests with their own political considerations and sought to use the former grounds to suppress information which might have damaging political consequences. This gave rise to the phenomenon of whistle blowing. This involved a civil servant deliberately leaking information to bodies such as the media when he or she believed that the public's right to know superseded the concern of a government to keep such material secret.

WHISTLE BLOWING IN BRITAIN

One example of whistle blowing occurred in Britain in the 1980s. Clive Ponting, a civil servant, leaked a document concerning the sinking of the Argentine cruiser, the *General Belgrano*, during the Falklands War to a Labour Member of Parliament, Mr. Tam Dalyell. He justified his action by arguing that the government was misleading Parliament and hence the country. He perceived that his duty to the nation as a public servant outweighed his loyalty to the government. Civil servants who engage in this activity run the risk of dismissal and imprisonment. Ponting was charged with breaking the Official Secrets Act but was acquitted in 1985 by a jury sympathetic to his arguments.

A danger posed by this activity is that it erodes the trust between ministers and civil servants. It might result in the politicisation of the bureaucracy whereby politicians appoint persons to its upper ranks whose trust and loyalty can be relied upon.

In 1989 a new Official Secrets Act was enacted in Britain. The sanction of a criminal prosecution was limited to certain categories of official information which were broadly associated with the interests of the state. Within these categories, an absolute ban was imposed on disclosure of some information (for example by intelligence officers discussing the operations of the security services) while in other areas (such as defence) it would be necessary to demonstrate that the disclosure resulted in 'harm' or 'jeopardy' to state interests. The Act contained no public interest defence which might be used by civil servants or investigative journalists who publicised government activities in these restricted areas.

The 'alternative' machinery of government

By what methods other than government departments can public policy be administered?

Our discussion has primarily been concerned with the work performed by civil servants in government departments. However, bureaucrats working for national governments are employed in organisations other than central departments. In most countries there exists a vast range of alternative mechanisms whereby national public policy is discharged.

In America regulatory agencies, government corporations and independent executive agencies perform federal government functions. In Britain a range of bodies which include QUANGOs (quasi autonomous non-governmental organisations) deliver services at both national and sub-national levels. In Ireland state sponsored bodies or semi-state bodies discharge important areas of central government work. The staff employed in this 'alternative machinery' of government may be civil servants but often are not.

The main advantage arising from the use of such machinery is that it is implemented by organisations which are purpose-built to perform a specific function. It does not have to accord to the organisation and structure dictated by normal civil service requirements. Thus people can be recruited with expertise which would not normally be possessed by civil servants (for example experience in conducting a large-scale business enterprise) and rewarded by a salary which does not have to conform to civil service pay scales. In both Britain and Ireland such bodies have been used to link the public and private sectors. There are two major problems affecting them.

Accountability

The extent to which these bodies are adequately accountable for their actions has been questioned. Such may be deliberately used to avoid the constant 'interference' of politicians. It is argued that organisations which pursue commercial activities require a certain amount of freedom so that enterprise can flourish. Others which pursue non-economic tasks may also justify a relative degree of insulation from political control on the grounds that the task with which they are concerned should not be subject to the constant to and fro of political debate: thus such bodies effectively depoliticise the function with which they are concerned. However, accountability remains an important issue as such bodies are concerned with the administration of public policy. Additionally some rely on state funding to finance all or some of their activities.

Accountability may be secured in three ways – by the chairperson (a political appointee) reporting to the minister, by the chief executive (a paid official) reporting to the department which is associated with the body (perhaps in the form of an annual report or a corporate plan indicating targets and performance) or through scrutiny exercised by the legislature over the operations which such bodies perform.

The consideration of annual reports might aid legislative scrutiny of such bodies but Parliamentary select committees (such as the Irish Joint Committee on State Sponsored Bodies, established in 1976) possibly possess greater potential for enabling legislatures to effectively examine the activities of these bodies.

Patronage

The second problem associated with the implementation of public policy by bodies other than government departments concerns the manner whereby those who manage these organisations are appointed. This has become a particular source of political debate in Britain during the 1990s when it has been alleged that the main criterion for the appointment of managers of such organisations has been their political sympathy for the government which appoints them. This led the Nolan Committee to recommend that appointments to quangos should be scrutinised by an independent commissioner.

Questions

1   List the main national government departments of any country with which you are familiar. Does this list suggest that any formula has been applied to determine the way in which the work of government is divided between these departments?
2   'It is inevitable that senior civil servants rather than ministers will dominate the policy-making process.' Do you agree with this statement? Can you see any problems which may arise as a result of such a situation?
3   'The civil service is a hierarchical organisation which utilises common structures such as grades and classes.' With reference to any country with which you are familiar, prepare a diagram to illustrate the way in which the civil service is organised.
4   Do you envisage that any problems may arise when private sector organisations implement public policy?

Summary

1 Much of the work of the executive branch of government is performed by paid officials. These are termed 'bureaucrats' and are often employed as civil servants subject to common conditions governing matters such as pay and conditions. The role of civil servants is to give advice to political members of the executive branch of government and to implement policy.

2 Many civil servants work in government departments. The organisation of these may be subject to alteration by the chief executive. The example of Britain suggests that although attempts might be made to organise government departments according to a logical formula, other considerations (including political constraints) influence their construction.

3 In theory politicians determine policy and civil servants implement it. But this theoretical division of responsibilities does not operate in practice and it is sometimes argued that civil servants dominate the policy-making process. This may be due to the expertise and permanence enjoyed by such officials. Some ministers may acquiesce to such a situation: those who do not, it has been alleged, will find the civil service manipulative and/or obstructive. In many countries attempts have been made to secure political control over the operations of civil servants through the use of personal advisers or through political involvement in senior civil service appointments.

4 It is sometimes alleged that the influence exerted by civil servants over policy making extends further and that civil servants with exclusive social backgrounds, education and training possess the ability to imbue society as a whole with their attitudes and beliefs. Acting in this capacity they are termed a 'ruling elite'.

5 Civil service reform has been pursued vigorously in many liberal democracies which experienced increases in the volume of state activity after 1945. The cost of the bureaucracy is one explanation of this. Reforms have typically included attempts to secure improved value for money, the separation of policy planning from its administration, and privatisation. In Britain the establishment of agencies to implement policy has been a key feature of reform but the resultant imperfect accountability of ministers for public policy has led to criticism.

6 Official secrecy often hampers the ability of members of the general

public to be fully aware of the activities performed by governments in their name. In Britain this has given rise to the phenomenon of 'whistle blowing'.

7 Bureaucrats may be employed in bodies other than government departments. In Britain QUANGOs have been widely used to administer public policy. Although this enables purpose-built bodies to discharge specific functions, such developments have been criticised on grounds of imperfect accountability and patronage.

10
THE LEGISLATIVE BRANCH OF GOVERNMENT

Functions

What roles do legislatures perform?

Elected legislatures are usually viewed as the symbol of representative government: as it is not possible for all citizens to directly share in policy making, they elect persons who perform these duties on their behalf. These representatives convene in the country's legislature. This is thus the institution which links the government and the governed. Additionally, legislatures undertake a number of specific tasks which we consider below.

Law making

Legislatures constitute the law-making body within a country's system of government. Thus making the law (or amending or repealing it) is a key function which they perform. A specific, although important, aspect of this role is approving the budget and granting authority for the collection of taxes. Below we consider the process of law making in Britain.

Law making in Britain
In Britain there is a difference between public and private legislation. The former constitutes the general law of the land but the latter is limited in jurisdiction (often being promoted by public bodies such as local authorities to extend their powers). A number of stages are involved in translating a proposal into law. The following outline applies to public legislation. We are assuming that this legislation is

first introduced into the House of Commons, which is generally (but not exclusively) the case.

First Reading: This is merely the announcement of an intention to introduce legislation on a particular topic. No debate occurs at this stage.

Second Reading: This is a debate on the general principles embodied in the legislative proposal (which is termed a 'bill'). If these principles are approved the bill progresses to the next stage in the legislative process.

Committee Stage: This involves a detailed examination of the contents of the bill. Amendments can be made provided that they do not destroy the bill's fundamental principles which have been approved in the second reading.

    This stage usually takes place in a standing committee which involves a relatively small number of MPs, although a committee of the whole House or a select committee may be used instead.

Report Stage: Changes to the bill proposed by the committee are considered by the full House of Commons and either approved or rejected.

Third Reading: This is a consideration of the bill as amended in its progress through the House of Commons.

If the bill receives its third reading, it then goes through a similar process in the House of Lords.

If amendments are proposed by the House of Lords, these need to be separately considered by the House of Commons which does, however, have paramountcy.

When such differences are dealt with, the bill is passed for Royal Assent. This is granted automatically, but is the process by which the 'bill' becomes an 'act'.

Scrutiny of the executive

Legislatures also scrutinise the actions of the executive branch of government. Governments are required to justify their actions to the legislature which may thus exert influence over the government's conduct. In some cases the legislature is required to give its consent to an action which the executive branch wishes to undertake. In America, for example, Congress has to approve a declaration of war.

In parliamentary systems in which the legislature provides the personnel of government, scrutiny facilitates ministerial responsibility. Governments are collectively responsible to the legislature. Perceived deficiencies in the overall activities of the government may result in its dismissal by the legislature (usually through the mechanism of a vote of 'no confidence'). Ministers may also be individually responsible for the performance of specific aspects of the work of the executive branch.

INDIVIDUAL MINISTERIAL RESPONSIBILITY

The ability of legislatures to force individual ministers to resign varies. In Germany, for example, the *Bundestag* lacks such a sanction. However, criticism by the legislature of a minister may result in that person's resignation.

In presidential systems the legislature may also have some ability to hold members of the executive branch accountable for their actions. In America, for example, Congress has a judicial power, that of impeachment. This is a formal charge that an official has committed an offence while in office. The charge results in a trial by the Senate which if proved would lead to that person's dismissal.

Legislatures may further be empowered to approve the nomination of members of the administration put forward by the chief executive. This applies to both parliamentary systems of government (such as Ireland) and also to presidential ones. In America, the Senate is required to confirm a wide range of presidential appointments.

Investigatory functions

The investigation of issues of public importance is a major function of many legislative bodies. This may be separate from exercising scrutiny over the actions of the executive. In America Congress has the right to summon witnesses to give evidence on a wide range of topics. Select committees may perform similar functions in countries such as Britain with parliamentary systems of government.

Raising issues of local and national importance

Legislatures debate policy and other issues of public importance. Such debates are published in official journals and through the media thus providing a source of information for the general public. This enables the electorate to be politically informed and educated. These bodies further provide a forum in which representatives can advance the interests of their constituencies and intercede on behalf of any of their constituents who have encountered problems in their dealings with the executive branch of government. Much work of this nature takes place in private, but it is usually possible to raise such issues publicly, within the legislative chamber.

Operations

How do legislatures perform their functions?

Debate

Legislatures are first and foremost debating institutions. This means that functions such as the consideration of legislation, the articulation of constituency issues or the discussion of matters of national importance are performed orally. Members of the legislature deliver speeches in which they put forward their views and listen to the judgments of their fellow legislators on the same issue. To facilitate debate, members of legislative bodies may enjoy certain immunities which ordinary members of the general public do not possess. In Britain, for example, Members of the House of Commons enjoy freedom of speech. This is one of a number of 'parliamentary privileges'. This means that in Parliament, Members may effectively say what they want (subject to the Speaker's rulings) to facilitate the maximum degree of openness in debate. Speeches made within Parliament by a Member, no matter how defamatory, cannot be subject to an action for slander.

Committees

Much of the work performed by contemporary legislative bodies is delegated to committees. In turn, these bodies may devolve responsibilities to sub-committees. These are useful devices because they enable a legislature to consider a number of matters at the same time and thus cope with the increased volumes of work associated with the expanded role of the state in the years following the Second World War and membership of supra-national bodies. They further enable small groups of legislators to investigate the affairs of government in considerable detail and through their reports the entire assembly becomes more knowledgeable about these matters and thus less dependent on government for the provision of information.

There are various types of committees existing in modern legislatures. In the British House of Commons a key division is between standing committees (which are used to consider legislation) and select committees (which are used for various purposes, including examination of the work performed by key government departments). A similar division exists in the American Congress. Both houses of Congress have a wide array of standing committees which consider bills in different policy areas. Select committees may be set up to investigate special problems. One example of this was the Senate Select Committee on Campaign Practices, which was established in 1973 to investigate the Watergate break-in. In countries whose legislatures consist of more than one chamber, joint committees may be established to enable the two chambers to cooperate for specific purposes.

Committees are an especially useful means for considering legislation. In countries such as America the examination of legislative proposals is aided by the system of hearings in which the committee or sub-committee considering the proposal invites interested parties to give evidence before it to ensure that their decisions are based on a diverse range of informed opinion. The decision whether to report a measure out of committee with a favourable recommendation or to 'kill' it is influenced by this procedure.

In some countries the work of committees extends beyond the consideration of legislative proposals. Legislation may be initiated by these bodies. The committee system of the German Parliament is particularly influential in this respect. Much of the work of the *Bundestag* is carried out through specialised committees whose areas of activity correspond to the federal ministries. These committees provide a forum in which ministers, civil servants and members of parliament (including those of the opposition parties) jointly engage in the process of policy making.

In addition to performing functions in relation to legislation, committees perform other tasks. In America they are also concerned with monitoring the bureaucracy and the manner in which policy is administered. This is termed 'oversight'.

LEGISLATIVE COMMITTEES AND THE PARTY SYSTEM

The party system may have an important bearing on the effectiveness with which committees operate in modern legislatures. The appointment of members to committees usually involves the party leadership and the fact that committee members are affiliated to a political party may influence the manner in which issues before a committee are viewed by its members.

In parliamentary systems such as the British, the party system may help the executive branch dominate committee proceedings since the governing party usually posseses a majority on committees considering legislation. In presidential systems such as the American, committees may exercise a far greater degree of autonomy since the executive branch is not directly involved in appointments. There appointments are allocated by the party apparatus which exists in both Houses although a member's desire to serve on a particular committee may be taken into account. Membership is not confined to a particular session of Congress: once appointed to a committee a member will usually remain on it for the remainder of his or her career. The chairmanship of such bodies is largely – although not now exclusively – determined by seniority.

Questions

In parliamentary systems of government, a further method of transacting business is through questions. These may be oral or written and are addressed to members of the executive branch of government. These can be of use in eliciting information, clarifying an issue or seeking to secure action by the executive branch of government, although they are rarely of importance to the process of policy making. In the British House of Commons the supplementary question is viewed as a major device seeking to catch members of the executive offguard. In the German *Bundestag* questions aid the process of ministerial accountability. The oral questioning of a minister may be followed by a vote which enables members of the legislature to express whether they are satisfied with the answers with which they have been provided.

The changing role of legislatures

What factors account for changes in the ability of legislatures to perform their traditional functions effectively ?

The effectiveness of legislatures varies from one country to another and is affected by constitutional or procedural rules governing the powers and conduct of legislatures which are unique to each country. In Britain, for example, scrutiny is aided by the opposition parties being granted a number of occasions during each parliamentary session when they may initiate debates which can be used to probe the actions of the executive. These are termed 'Supply Days'. But such facilities do not universally exist in legislatures with a parliamentary system of government.

It is argued that legislatures do not adequately perform the functions which we referred to above. Several factors might explain this.

Membership of supra-national bodies

The membership of supra-national bodies has implications for both the law-making and scrutinising roles performed by national legislatures. In Britain, for example, membership of the European Union has resulted in the loss of some of Parliament's traditional legislative functions but has also added to the volume of governmental activity which this body is expected to monitor.

Developments affecting 'direct democracy'

The use which many liberal democracies now make of referendums, the ability of some pressure groups to further their objectives by securing permanent access to the executive branch of government and the ability of chief executives to act independently of legislatures in certain circumstances have all tended to result in legislatures being bypassed as the arena within which public policy is initiated.

The role of the media

The ability of the legislature to scrutinise the actions of the executive, to air grievances or to educate the public concerning political affairs is often more effectively conducted by the media. Investigative journalism, in particular, may secure the accomplishment of these roles.

Domination by the executive branch of government

A major explanation which is offered for changes in the effectiveness of legislatures to perform their traditional functions is the tendency for such bodies to be dominated by the executive branch of government. In many countries the initiation of policy and the control over finance has passed to the executive branch. In Britain, for example, the bulk of public legislation is initiated by the government. Parliament responds to the agenda set by the government. It may subsequently be able to influence the detailed content of such legislation but is not the driving force behind it. Additionally, governments may be able to utilise procedural devices to expedite the progress of their legislation. In Britain one such device is the guillotine. This is a procedural mechanism which limits the time devoted to a debate which ensures that the progress of a government measure is not halted by unnecessary or excessive parliamentary scrutiny.

This situation of executive dominance of the legislature has occurred in both parliamentary and presidential systems of government. There are two reasons which might account for this development. The first concerns the volume of post-war state activity, much of which is of a complex and technical nature. This has made it difficult for members of legislatures to keep abreast of the affairs of modern government and has tended to result in ministers and civil servants within the executive branch exercising a dominant position in policy making because of the superior information which they have at their disposal.

The second explanation for executive dominance of legislatures is the development of the party system. The party system possesses some obvious advantages for legislative bodies. It helps to prevent legislative anarchy (in the sense of members seeking to pursue individual interests to the exclusion of all else) and organises the work of such bodies thus ensuring that specific goals and objectives are achieved. But there are also disadvantages for legislatures which arise from the party system. It aligns members of the executive and legislative branches. Members of both branches, when belonging to the same party, have common ideological and policy interests. They have a vested interest in successfully translating these common concerns into law. Such mutual interests are underlaid by party discipline which serves to induce members of the legislature to follow the lead given by their party leaders within the executive branch of government. In extreme cases where party discipline is strong, disobedience to the wishes of the executive might result in expulsion from the party, a fate which befell the British Conservative Party 'Eurorebels' in 1994.

The emergence of disciplined political parties has the effect of ensuring that legislatures do not act as corporate institutions exercising their functions on behalf of the nation as a whole. Instead they operate under the direction of the executive branch of government.

EXECUTIVE–LEGISLATURE RELATIONS IN FRANCE

The emergence of disciplined political parties has been especially apparent in France. The situation of governments being placed at the mercy of constantly shifting coalitions in the National Assembly has been replaced by the development of parties organised in support of or opposition to the government. This situation is termed *le fait majoritaire*. It supplemented other developments contained in the 1958 constitution which were designed to subordinate the legislature to the executive. These included limitations on the ability of the National Assembly to dismiss governments and facilities for governments to secure the passage of legislation lacking majority support in either the National Assembly or the Senate.

Adversarial politics

The operations of the party system have one further consequence which may devalue the workings of the legislature. Party systems often give rise to adversarial politics. Britain and New Zealand are examples of countries whose political affairs are traditionally conducted in this manner.

Adversarial politics denotes a situation in which one party is automatically disposed to oppose the views and suggestions of another as a point of principle. If this style of politics influences the operations of the legislature, it means that this body lacks any sense of common purpose. The work of the legislature is less concerned with a genuine search for the best solutions to issues and problems regardless of party affiliation but is mainly activated by the furtherance of partisan acrimony and the pursuit of party advantage. Members of the legislature who are supporters of the same party from which the executive is drawn are likely to back that government and deride proposals made by the opposition party (or parties) regardless of the merits of the cases put forward. Similarly, those who are not supporters of the government are likely to make destructive rather than constructive assessments of initiatives put forward by the executive branch.

Thus party systems may erode the ability of legislatures to take dispassionate consideration of a range of ideas and then support those which overall opinion within that body agrees is the best course of action in the national interest.

LEGITIMISING

If the initiative in proposing legislation is passed to the executive branch of government which then controls the progress of that legislation through the workings of the party system, the legislature is greatly devalued as an institution. Its main role becomes not that of making law but of confirming decisions that have been reached elsewhere (for example in cabinet meetings or in inter-party discussions).

Nonetheless, when passed by the legislature, the law applies to all citizens who are required to obey it. Compliance is most effectively achieved by downplaying the political forces which have shaped legislation and associating it with the actions of a body whose authority is widely acknowledged. Law is therefore depicted as the outcome of a process engaged in by the entire legislative body: legislation is viewed as the collective decision of this assembly which is ultimately responsible to the people.

Legitimising thus entails enhancing the status of the actions of the government. The power of the latter is augmented with the authority of parliament thereby ensuring wide public compliance to the government's measures.

Public confidence

To what extent and why has public confidence in legislatures suffered in recent years?

A consideration of changes affecting contemporary legislatures should extend beyond a consideration of the problems which such bodies face in performing their traditional functions. We must also consider arguments which allege the aura and prestige of these institutions has suffered in recent years.

The economic climate

Public confidence in legislatures may be especially affected by the economic climate. Factors such as recession are likely to have an adverse impact on the way the public view all institutions of government, especially when it appears that they have no instant solutions to contemporary problems. Recession is likely to further reduce the capacity of institutions of government to act as innovators: rather than act as dynamic proponents of reform (which may enhance the standing of such bodies in the public eye) both executives and legislators are disposed towards inaction and to pruning public spending. This is a less adventurous exercise than initiating new programmes and may have an adverse effect on the way in which the public view the machinery of government.

Performance of diverse functions

We have also seen that legislatures perform a wide range of functions. However, not all of these are compatible. In particular prominent attention to the role of promoting local considerations may detract from the legislature's ability to exercise superintendence over national affairs and provide the appearance of a fragmented body with no overall sense of purpose. This may also result in the decline of the aura and prestige of that body.

This argument has been presented in connection with the American Congress where, it is argued, the parochialism of its members detracts from that body's ability or willingness to view matters from an overall national perspective. Although American Congressional elections are fought by candidates who represent the nation's major parties, the main influence on the outcome of these elections is the personal vote which a candidate can attract. This personal vote may be secured on the basis of that person's campaigning style and how they 'come across' to local voters. However, the key basis of a personal vote is the candidate's previous record when in office. This record can be based on factors which include accessibility to local constituents (especially the provision of help to those with problems), the voicing of support for local interests or causes and particularly the ability to attract government resources into the constituency which the candidate represents. It follows, therefore, that incumbent candidates (that is, those who are striving for re-election) are in a far better position to win seats in the House of Representatives or Senate than is a candidate who has no record to advance and is seeking to win a seat for the first time. Only factors such as a dilatory record in advancing constituency interests or being involved in some form of scandal are likely to offset the incumbent's advantage. Although sitting candidates do sometimes lose, a key feature of elections to Congress is that incumbents are in a good position to win, and usually do so.

It has been argued that this situation results in Congress having a dual character: it is at one and the same time a body composed of politicians with a keen interest (or even a preoccupation) with local affairs but is also a forum for making national policy. Concern with the former consideration may detract from the latter function and reduce Congress's effectiveness in responding to current or future problems.

PAROCHIALISM

The role which legislators perform in providing a service to their constituents is an important one in many countries. In Ireland members of the Dáil are often prominent participants in the local political affairs of the constituency they represent and view the promotion of local interests and articulation of individual grievances as roles which are of more importance than formulating national legislation. Even ministers are not immune from these parochial pressures.

In Britain reference is often made to a Member of Parliament's 'personal vote'. By this we mean that some candidates secure support from their local electors on the basis of who they are and what they have done (especially in connection with the service provided to their constituents). Such support is, however, far less important than a candidate's party label.

The decline of legislatures?

Is the work performed by legislatures, therefore, destined to become insignificant?

In the above two sections we have referred to difficulties faced by contemporary legislatures. We have argued that they face two related sets of problems – the inability to discharge their traditional functions effectively and changes in public perceptions of the aura and prestige of such bodies. These arguments can be amalgamated into the suggestion that there has been a decline in legislatures.

However, although we have charted major developments which have contributed to arguments alleging the decline of such bodies, it is important to appreciate that they continue to perform valuable and vital roles in political affairs. Some of the problems to which we have drawn attention are neither universal nor insuperable. For example, the dominant hold which governments exercise over the law-making process is greater in some countries than in others. In both Germany and Italy, for example, there remains a considerable degree of scope for legislation to be initiated by ordinary (or 'backbench') members of the legislature.

We have drawn attention to the impact of the party system on the role of legislatures. However, the strength of party varies from one liberal democracy to another and this has an obvious bearing on the subservience of the legislature to the executive. For example, the nature of the American party relationship between Congress and the president is one factor which explains why Congress has retained an extremely significant role in law making. Additionally, the dominance which governments possess over the conduct of legislatures through the operations of the party system is not always a constant feature in the political affairs of a country. There are occasions when legislatures may assert themselves to a greater degree. This is when (in a parliamentary system) no one party possesses overall majority support in the legislature or when (in a presidential system) the executive branch of government is controlled by a different party than that which controls the legislature.

LEGISLATURE ASSERTIVENESS – SOME EXAMPLES

In Ireland during the 1980s the absence of one party with an overall majority gave the Dáil the opportunity to exercise its right to dismiss governments. Two were dismissed and a third was forced to resign and seek a dissolution.

When the presidency and National Assembly in France were controlled by different political parties during the period of 'cohabitation' (1986–88 and 1993–95), the president was forced to appoint a prime minister who enjoyed the support of the National Assembly. This implied that governments were accountable to the legislature rather than to the president.

The November 1994 American Congressional elections resulted in the Democratic party losing its majority in both the House of Representatives and the Senate. This enabled Congress to seize the initiative from President Clinton in major policy areas, especially in the area of public expenditure.

Thus the party system is a double-edged sword. Although it sometimes aids executive dominance over the legislature, it may also enable legislatures to assert themselves at the expense of executive power. Their ability to do this may further be enhanced by reforms which we discuss in the following section.

The role of select committees

Legislatures may seek to provide themselves with mechanisms designed to elicit information on the affairs of government, thus enhancing that body's ability to effectively scrutinise the actions of the government. Individual legislators may be provided with financial aid to employ staff, one of whose roles could be to provide expert knowledge of specific policy areas. British Members of Parliament and members of the Irish Dáil are extremely poorly served in this respect while American legislators fare far better, with large personal staffs and the support of expert research services.

Select committees constitute a key reform to facilitate legislative scrutiny of the affairs of government. Their deliberations provide a source of information which is separate from that provided by the executive branch. Further, the non-partisan climate within which select committee discussions are held may reduce the domination exerted by the executive branch of government thereby enhancing the status of the legislature. This has been the case in Ireland, France, Britain, New Zealand and Canada.

In Britain, the Public Accounts Committee was an early example of a select committee which monitored the work of government. Specifically it examined the accounts of government departments and sought to ensure that money voted by Parliament was spent effectively and for the purposes which Parliament had agreed. Its work is aided by the Comptroller and Auditor-General and the National Audit Office. In 1979 a new system of select committees was introduced into the House of Commons to monitor the work performed by all the key government departments. Such bodies were designed to make all MPs more informed concerning the work of government. To aid them in their deliberations, such committees were empowered to hire staff with expertise in the area of government with which they were concerned and to secure evidence from persons who were not MPs but who possessed knowledge of the subject area under discussion. This reform was not universally welcomed, however. Some politicians feared that the power of these committees would further devalue Parliament as an institution. Key legislative functions would be transferred to committees. It was also argued that these bodies would promote consensus politics since committee members would feel pressurised to compromise their views in order to produce a unanimous report.

In Ireland, the *Fine Gael*–Labour coalition (1982–87) established a number of select committees in 1983 but most of them were abandoned by the *Fianna Fáil* government in 1987. Major reforms to the system of select committees were introduced into the New Zealand parliament by the in-coming Labour government in 1985. These reforms were designed to subject the process of government to enhanced parliamentary and public scrutiny. One significant innovation was the power of such committees to inquire on their own initiative into any area of government administration, policy or spending.

Relations within the legislative branch of government

Why do legislatures usually consist of more than one body?

In most liberal democratic political systems the legislature is divided into two separate bodies. These bodies form separate debating chambers. For example, in Britain Parliament consists of the House of Commons and the House of Lords. In America the legislative branch is divided into the House of Representatives and the Senate. In Ireland, Parliament (the *Oireachtas*) consists of the *Dáil Éireann* and the *Seanad Éireann* while in France the legislative function of government is shared between the National Assembly and the Senate. In the new Republic of South Africa, the legislature is divided into a 400-member National Assembly and a 90-member Senate. These countries have what is termed a bicameral legislature.

The opposite of this is a unicameral system in which the legislature consists of only one body. Examples of this are found in New Zealand, Finland and Denmark. In 1970 Sweden also abandoned its bicameral system and replaced it with a unicameral one.

Below we consider the advantages of having a legislature composed of two bodies.

A revising chamber

One main benefit of a bicameral legislature is that one chamber can give the other an opportunity to think again, to reconsider its position. On occasions when the content of legislation is contentious and the period surrounding its passage through the first of the legislative bodies is charged with emotion for and against the measure, it is useful that a second chamber can coolly and calmly reevaluate what has been done and if necessary invite the first chamber to reassess the situation by either rejecting the measure or proposing amendments to it. In this case the second performs the function of a revising chamber.

Differences in composition

In bicameral systems, the two chambers of the legislature are often composed in different ways. This may also be an advantage in that it enables issues to be examined from different perspectives. Thus in

Britain the House of Commons is elected by popular vote whereas the House of Lords consists of persons who are members by birth (hereditary peers), nomination (life peers) or by virtue of holding high office in the Church of England (the lords spiritual) or the judiciary (the law lords).

In some countries one chamber of the legislature is designed to represent public opinion while the other is concerned with territorial representation - advancing the more localised views of the areas, states or regions into which the country is divided. This was originally the justification for creating the American Senate. When the constitution was being drafted a conflict of interest emerged between the sparsely populated states and those in which large numbers of persons resided. Thus the constitution adopted a compromise position (which was termed the 'Connecticut Compromise'). This resulted in representation in one chamber (the House of Representatives) being based on population, which would give the populous states a greater voice in that body. However each state, regardless of size, was given equal representation in the second chamber, the Senate. The Australian Parliament also consists of two chambers, the House of Representatives and the Senate. The latter's role is to represent the states, with each being allotted 10 members. A key role of the South African Senate is to exercise responsibility for regional affairs. To facilitate this, each provincial legislature, regardless of size, elects 10 senators to this body.

BICAMERALISM IN GERMANY AND FRANCE

In Germany the *Bundestag* consists of representatives elected by the voters whereas the *Bundesrat* provides a forum at national level in which the views of the states (or *Länder*) can be put forward. Each state sends delegations to this body who are mandated to act in accordance with the instructions given to them by the state government. Each state is allotted three votes in the *Bundesrat*, with extra votes being given to the more populated states.

The second chamber in France, the Senate, also possesses a strong base in the localities. Its members are elected for a term of nine years by an electoral college which is composed of deputies of the National Assembly and local politicians drawn from the *départements* and city councils. Local influences are further reflected in the National Assembly many of whose members are local politicians, serving as mayors or regional councillors.

Functional representation

Second chambers may also articulate concerns other than territorial ones. They may represent the interests of specific groups within a country. This is referred to as functional representation. The Irish *Seanad* is theoretically constituted in part on this basis. Members of this body are not directly elected but are supposed to reflect vocational interests. The majority of its members are thus chosen from lists of candidates representing key vocational groups in Irish society (education and culture, agriculture, industry and commerce, labour and public administration and social services). An electoral college composed of members of local authorities and Parliament (the *Oireachtas*) then selects 43 Senators from these lists. A further six are chosen from graduates of the National University of Ireland and Dublin University and the Prime Minister (*Taoiseach*) appoints a further 11 members. In reality, however, party affiliation is the key for election to this body.

The resolution of disagreements in bicameral legislatures

When legislatures are composed of more than one chamber, how are disagreements resolved?

It is conceivable that disputes between the bodies which compose a bicameral legislature will sometimes arise. These situations are usually catered for in a country's constitution or by political practices which seek to avoid a situation in which one chamber effectively vetoes the work of the other, resulting in total inaction. Let us consider some examples.

In Ireland the resolution of disagreement is catered for by the constitution. This established the *Seanad* as an inferior body to the *Dáil* in terms of the functions which it performs. The latter body nominates the *Taoiseach* and approves the government. The government is responsible only to the *Dáil* and most legislation is introduced into this house. The *Seanad*'s subsidiary role thus minimises its ability to disrupt the process of government. In Britain too, the two chambers are not coequal in power. Thus in the case of disagreement between the two Houses of Parliament, the one with the elected base will ultimately prevail. This situation is enshrined in the 1949 Parliament Act which gives the House of Lords the power to delay the progress of non-financial legislation which has been passed by the House of Commons for the maximum period of one year, after which (provided the measure is re-introduced in the House of Commons) it will become law.

The French constitution provides for the pre-eminence of the National Assembly over the Senate. Only the former body can dismiss a government and it also possesses the ultimate ability to determine legislation, although in the event of disagreements between the two chambers an attempt will usually be made to seek a compromise. The Senate does, however, possess important powers (including the need to consent to changes in the constitution) and has on occasions asserted itself, especially during periods of socialist government when this party controlled the National Assembly. This situation is referred to as 'conflictual bicameralism'.

'PRE-STUDY' IN CANADA

One difficulty which may affect the operations of a bicameral legislature is the time available for a second chamber to adequately examine legislation sent to it by the first.

One solution to this is the process of 'pre-study' which has sometimes been utilised by the Canadian Senate since 1945. This is a process by which the subject matter of a bill under consideration in the House of Commons can be considered by a Senate committee at the same time. The report of this committee's deliberations is made available to the House of Commons which may consider the Senate's reactions to the proposal which is before them and if necessary introduce amendments before transmitting the bill to that body.

This process enables the Senate to examine legislation placed before them relatively quickly but also ensures that they are able to make a valid contribution to the law-making process by making their views on it known before it is formally sent to them for examination.

In America the two branches the legislature are equal in status. The institution of direct election for senators in 1913   resulted in both Houses of Congress being popularly elected. Disagreements between the two chambers on legislation are resolved through the mechanism of a Conference Committee. If a bill is passed in different versions by the two Houses a committee composed of members of each House is appointed to resolve the differences and draw up a single bill which is then returned to each House for a vote. Should either house reject this bill, it is returned to the Conference Committee for further deliberation. It is not necessary to resort to this mechanism frequently, but when it is used it may provide a forum in which 'trade-offs' between the House of Representatives and the Senate are made.

Questions

1 With reference to any legislature with which you are familiar, compile a list of its major functions. How are these functions carried out ?
2 Identify the main factors which have led to allegations of the 'decline of legislatures' since 1945. Is this a general problem affecting legislatures in liberal democracies ?
3 List what you consider to be the main strengths and weaknesses of bicameral legislatures.
4 Describe the stages involved in the law-making process in any legislature with which you are familiar. How effective do you consider this process to be?

Summary

1 Legislatures perform a number of functions in liberal democracies. These include making the law, scrutinising the actions of the executive, debating issues of public importance and serving as a forum in which representatives can raise issues on behalf of their constituencies or individual constituents.
2 Legislatures transact their affairs through a number of mechanisms including debate and questions. Wide use is made of committees.
3 It is sometimes argued that legislatures fail to carry out their traditional functions effectively. Developments in which legislation is initiated by supra-national bodies, pressure groups or the public

may help to account for this situation, but a major explanation is the dominance which the executive branch of government frequently exerts over legislatures. This is principally due to the development of the party system and the discipline with which this is associated. The party system has further given rise in many liberal democracies to a system of adversarial politics which influences the atmosphere within which legislatures operate.

4 Legislatures have also been affected by developments which have reduced the public standing of such bodies. The impact of recession (which limits the ability of legislatures to be dynamic innovators) and the excessive parochialism associated with some institutions (which restricts their ability to promote the national interest) help to account for the loss of prestige faced by some modern legislatures.

5 Points 3 and 4 have given rise to arguments which allege the 'decline' of modern legislatures.

6 Nonetheless, legislatures continue to perform vital functions in the political affairs of modern liberal democracies. The hold which the executive branch exerts over legislatures and the strength of the party system are factors subject to considerable variation both between liberal democracies and even within one country over periods of time. Legislatures thus often possess the ability to assert themselves in relation to the executive branch of government and their ability to do so has been enhanced by reforms which include the development of the select committee system.

7 In most liberal democratic political systems, legislatures are bicameral bodies consisting of two separate chambers. One may act as a revising chamber or be constituted on a different basis to the other thus allowing differing perspectives to be deployed in the transaction of the work of the legislature. One problem which may arise is disagreement between the two chambers although this situation is often resolved by one chamber having an inferior status to the other.

11
THE JUDICIARY AND LAW ENFORCEMENT

Political considerations affecting the work of the courts and the police

Why is the operation of a country's system of law enforcement of interest to students of politics?

For a system of law enforcement to be accepted as legitimate within any particular country it must be seen as impartial. This is most easily guaranteed when the agencies engaged in the system of law enforcement (especially the courts and the police) are free from political pressures and biases and thus able to apply the law in the same manner to all persons within a country. However, total freedom from political pressures or involvement is impossible in any system of government. The courts and the police do not operate in a vacuum. These bodies are subject to political pressures and the role they perform and the decisions which they make may project them forcibly into the arena of politics.

POLITICAL INVOLVEMENT IN THE JUDICIAL SYSTEM

Politicians may involve themselves in the workings of the judicial system.

In Britain, for example, the belief that the Home Secretary was blocking moves to consider the parole of long-serving IRA prisoners led five of them, in 1995, to successfully secure the permission of the High Court to challenge the delays which

---

> had occurred in hearing their applications. In Ireland the release of 12 IRA prisoners in July 1995 was intended as a means of maintaining the momentum of the peace process.

Thus as students of politics we need to be aware of the nature of the work performed by the police and the courts. We also need to consider the extent to which their activities are influenced by political considerations and the way in which the work they perform has significance for the manner in which political issues are resolved.

General issues affecting the control and accountability of the police

Who should exercise control over the police and to whom should the police be accountable for their actions?

We are familiar with the sight of police officers patrolling our neighbourhoods on foot or in cars. Their main role is to ensure that all citizens obey the law. If they fail to do so the police can invoke a range of sanctions. These may include cautioning or arresting a person who is breaking the law. But we need to ensure that the police carry out their duties fairly and impartially. These objectives highlight the importance of the mechanisms which exist for the exercise of control over police work and through which the police can be made to account for their actions. These are important issues in liberal democratic systems of government. There are three main options for us to examine.

National government control of police work

If a police force is controlled by, and accountable to, national government there is a danger that the main role of that organisation will be to promote the political interests of the party or parties from which the government is formed. Typically the government will identify its interests with those of the state. Thus police operations might be directed by the national government or legislation might be interpreted for the police by that government. The police are then answerable to this body for the manner in which they have discharged their duties. The police therefore personify the state. They are the 'state in uniform'. Such a situation existed, for example, when South Africa was subject to white minority rule.

NATIONAL CONTROL OF POLICING

In France central government performs a major role in police affairs. There are two main police forces. The *Police nationale* is controlled by the Ministry of the Interior while the *Gendarmerie nationale* is technically part of the armed forces under the control of the Ministry of Defence. Officers from these bodies are also used as investigating officers to conduct enquiries under the supervision of an investigating judge or a public prosecutor. In this capacity they are termed the *Police judiciaire* and are responsible to the judiciary.

In Ireland the *Garda Síochána* operates on a national scale, controlled by a commissioner appointed by the Minister of Justice to whom the commissioner is theoretically responsible.

The main danger which might arise from such a close identification between the police and national government concerns the style of policing. If the main role of the police is to uphold the interests of the government, policing may be coercive in nature, directed against all those who disagree with the policies pursued by that government. Coercive policing may be pursued by paramilitary police bodies who take their orders from a minister in the national government. Their attitude may be that of 'shoot first and ask questions later' since there is no body other than the government to hold the police accountable for their actions.

Local government control of policing

A second possibility is that the police should be subject to local control. This may be performed by state governments, local authorities or by the direct election of police chiefs. The police would then be accountable at local level for their activities. This would ensure that a number of police forces operated within the country. It may thus guard against police work being concerned with the advancement of the interests of one particular political party (or group of parties acting in alliance). It is likely that a range of political parties will exercise control over the large number of state or local governments found in any one country. This will prevent police work from being primarily directed towards one overriding political aim.

In this situation police work can be orientated towards issues felt to be of concern to ordinary members of the general public. Police activity is directed towards matters such as responding to crime and lawlessness rather than towards achieving the political priorities of national government. This role is appreciated by the public who support the police in their work. Policing is thus carried out with the consent of most members of the population.

CONTROL OF AMERICAN POLICING

In America policing is primarily a local affair, controlled by local government operating at county or municipal levels. The national guard which exists at state level may also perform police-related functions. Additionally the Federal Bureau of Investigation is an agency of the justice department with the responsibility of enforcing federal laws. Local control, however, does not necessarily take the politics out of policing. State or local governments also have political objectives which they wish to fulfil and the police may be used to further these.

The development of urban policing in America, for example, was considerably influenced by local politics in which jobs and promotion in police forces and the tasks which the police fulfilled were greatly influenced by local politicians. Lack of efficiency and even corruption stemmed from this situation, which persisted for a number of decades in the late nineteenth and early twentieth centuries.

Professional control of policing

A final option is that police work should be controlled by, and accountable to, those professionals who actually perform the work. Under this model, senior police officers in charge of police forces exercise control over such bodies and individual police officers are accountable for their actions to these commanders. This system of control and accountability might seem the best guarantee of political impartiality in the exercise of police work. It leaves the police free to determine what are the most important functions to discharge and thereby enhance the trust and co-operation of the general public.

There are, however, problems with such a system. The police and the public may have different views concerning issues such as what matters should receive priority attention. There is the danger that the police and public may become so distanced that the role of the police is seen as illegitimate by citizens. It is also possible that members of the general public will distrust a system in which police officers are subject only to internal mechanisms of accountability. Remedies against abuse of power are difficult in a situation in which the police are a 'law unto themselves'. The British concept of constabulary independence perhaps comes closest to the model of police work being subjected to the control of senior police officers.

The British policing system

How effective is the 'tripartite' system of police accountability?

In this section we seek to examine the control and accountability of policing in one country in some detail.

The models we have examined in the above section imply that police accountability is most efficiently secured when control is in the hands of one body. But suppose control over police functions is shared between several bodies. Does such a situation have an advantageous or disadvantageous effect on the accountability of the police? To answer this question we will examine the British experience.

When the new system of British policing was developed in the early decades of the nineteenth century it was controlled by, and accountable to, local government. The exception to this was the Metropolitan police force (which was, and is, controlled by the Home Secretary). Elsewhere, policing was organisationally attached to local government and was supervised by a committee of councillors in urban areas (termed the watch committee) and by the magistrates in rural parts of Britain (who until 1888 exercised the functions of local government in such places).

As the century developed, however, others became involved in police affairs. The decision by central government to pay some of the costs of provincial police forces in 1856 was accompanied by a mechanism to ensure that each locality benefiting from such new financial arrangements conducted its police in an efficient manner. This was the inspectorate whose role was implemented by visiting each and every force.

The role of central government further increased when the size of the government grant to police forces was doubled in 1874 and was considerably strengthened when the 1919 Police Act made a number of issues (such as pay and conditions of work) subject to the central direction of the Home Office.

Additionally, chief constables also sought to carve out for themselves areas of control over police work. These people began to see themselves less as servants of the local authorities which employed them but, instead, as professionals who needed a certain degree of insulation from outside pressures in order to perform their work effectively. In the early decades of the twentieth century some of these officers were involved in disputes with their local authorities to determine who exercised control over police work. A landmark judicial decision, *Fisher* v. *Oldham Corporation* (1930) suggested that the unique common law derivation of the office of constable prevented bodies such as local authorities giving specific instructions to chief constables and the forces which they headed. Chief constables began to insist that they were accountable to the law but not to local or national politicians.

Thus by the middle of the twentieth century, control over police work was shared between three bodies: local government, national government (by both the Home Office and the Home Secretary) and by chief constables. The 1964 Police Act sought to regularise this situation by stipulating the precise areas of responsibilities attached to each of these. Outside of London, the role of local government was to be discharged by a new body, the police authority. This was normally a committee of a county council, whose boundaries, when re-modelled by the 1972 Local Government Act, provided the geographic basis for policing in England and Wales. This Act further introduced the tripartite system of police accountability. By this system certain aspects of the work controlled by one of these three bodies had to be referred to another for sanction or rejection. This was effectively a system of checks and balances which made one body accountable for the performance of some aspects of its work to one of the others.

THE TRIPARTITE SYSTEM OF POLICE ACCOUNTABILITY

We can understand how this system operated by considering the following two examples.

First, a chief constable was allocated the responsibility for the direction and control of his or her police force but the police authority could demand information from this official concerning the way in which an area was policed. Second, the power to appoint and dismiss chief constables was given to a police authority, but when it had made a decision the Home Secretary had the ultimate power to accept or reject it.

The system whereby one body was accountable for the performance of its work to one of the others was, however, a flawed system. The situation was complicated by the absence of effective sanctions which one body could deploy against another and also by the ability of one of them to avoid being held responsible for its actions by appealing to the third participant to the process. For example, a chief constable required by a police authority to produce a report on police activities could appeal to the Home Secretary to override the request.

The main problem, however, was that the allocation of functions between the three bodies responsible for exercising control over police work lacked precision. Each body was provided with generalised responsibilities but was largely left to determine their actual substance and detailed application. Such imprecision made it possible for one body to encroach on the work which another felt it was its duty to perform: further, the extent of this implied autonomy made it difficult to secure the adequate accountability of one body to another.

Initially disputes arose between some police authorities and their chief constables. These authorities argued that chief constables unilaterally implemented policies and paid insufficient attention to the views and requirement of local people. It was thus argued that police work should be more accountable to police authorities and thence to the general public. Arguments that friction between police and public could be partly attributed to the absence of effective mechanisms to make the police accountable for their actions to the general public resulted in some reforms, including the requirement (in the 1984 Police and Criminal Evidence Act) that regular consultative exercises should be conducted between the police and general public.

ABUSE OF POWER

In 1981 a series of disorders occurred in many of Britain's urban areas. One explanation given for these events was that the relationship between the police and public was deficient. There was a perception that some police officers abused their powers.

The government appointed an inquiry into these disorders, chaired by Lord Scarman. This reported in 1981 and was responsible for initiating a number of reforms to police recruitment and training policies designed to improve the relationship between the police and ethnic minority communities. Other reforms were included in the 1984 Police and Criminal Evidence Act.

The use of police powers including 'stop and search' on the streets became subject to safeguards which enabled an individual officer's conduct to be monitored. Further, the machinery used for investigating complaints by members of the public against police officers was reformed. The Police Complaints Board (established in 1976) was abolished and replaced by the Police Complaints Authority. Although outside investigation of complaints against the police was not instituted this new body was given the ability to supervise such police investigations.

However, the 1980s also witnessed a considerable increase in the control exercised by central government over police affairs. Arguments arose concerning the accountability of this body for its actions in connection with police affairs. The 1964 Police Act made the Home Secretary responsible for superintendence over the entire police service which potentially gave this politician great influence over policing. Additionally, however, other bodies (such as the Audit Commission) involved themselves in police matters in the Conservative governments' drive for efficiency and value for money throughout the entire public sector. The emphasis by the Citizens' Charter on consumerism also imposed outside constraints on the way in which policing was delivered.

The 1994 Police and Magistrates' Courts Act further enhanced the degree of control exerted by central government over police affairs.

Senior officers were placed upon fixed term contracts. Key national objectives and performance indicators were drawn up by the Home Office to emphasise the need for police actions to be accountable to central direction. The bulk of the finance for each police force was now provided by national government which set force budgets and also had the ability to subject them to cash limits. But there has, however, been very little debate concerning the mechanisms needed to ensure that central government is adequately accountable for the way in which it exercises its control over police work. Critics argue that central government has been given power without responsibility.

It might be argued that ideally, control over police work should be shared. Central government, state and/or local government and the police themselves all have a valid role to perform in determining the character, nature and orientation of police work. However, as the above account suggested, divided control does not necessarily provide an effective system of accountability.

The role of the courts

What do the courts do?

The main role of the courts is to adjudicate a dispute between two parties. These two parties may be private citizens who are in dispute with each other. Alternatively, the state may be party to a case which comes before the courts.

No two liberal democratic countries have an identical judicial system. Differences exist, in particular, in the conduct of trials. Britain and America utilise the adversarial system in which two parties seek to prove their case by discrediting that put forward by their opponents. The trial is presided over by a judge whose main function is to ensure fair play. Many European countries utilise an inquisitorial system. Here the gathering of evidence is the responsibility of the judge and the main function of the trial is to resolve issues uncovered in the earlier investigation. The judge will actively intervene in the trial in order to order to arrive at the truth.

Civil and criminal law

Civil law is concerned with the resolution of disagreements in which, typically, one party seeks some form of redress (such as damages) from a second party. Criminal law encompasses activities which have broader social implications and which thus require the state to initiate a prosecution with a view to punishing the offender. Slander is an example of a civil action: murder is a criminal charge.

In many countries civil and criminal matters are heard in different courts. This is not invariably the case, however. In France civil and criminal matters are heard in the one court, the *ordre judiciaire*, utilising the same judicial personnel. In Britain a circuit judge may hear both civil and criminal cases and magistrates' courts perform some civil functions.

THE ORGANISATION OF THE COURTS IN BRITAIN

The civil and criminal courts in Britain are organised in a hierarchical fashion.

Most criminal cases are tried in magistrates courts. The more serious, carrying heavier sentences, are heard in Crown Courts presided over by a judge and making use of a jury. Appeals against the verdicts reached in Crown Courts are heard by the Court of Appeal (Criminal Division).

Minor civil matters may be handled by the small claims procedure which seeks to resolve a dispute without the need to take it to open court. Most civil cases which go to court are heard by County Courts, although the High Court of Justice may hear cases in which large sums of money are claimed. Appeals against a verdict reached in a County Court or the High Court will be heard by the Court of Appeal (Civil Division).

The House of Lords is the final court of appeal for both criminal and civil cases.

Administrative law

Administrative law is concerned with the relationship between a government and its citizens. In Britain challenges mounted by the general public to the actions or operations of the executive branch of government may be heard in the courts. The legality of delegated legislation or accusations of abuse of power may be challenged in this manner. Minor issues (such as a challenge to a decision taken by a civil servant) may, however, be resolved by a tribunal. Complaints of maladministration (that is an accusation that incorrect procedures were followed to arrive at a decision) may be submitted to the Ombudsman.

In other countries, however, a separate court system exists to adjudicate upon such matters. Germany and France have a distinct system of courts concerned with administrative law.

THE FRENCH SYSTEM OF ADMINISTRATIVE COURTS

A belief that the executive branch of government would become subordinate to the judiciary if the ordinary courts were able to review actions undertaken by the executive resulted in the establishment of a separate system of Administrative Courts in France. These have exclusive jurisdiction in a wide range of cases covered by public law which involve disagreements between individuals and the workings of the state, including allegations of illegal actions undertaken by ministers, civil servants and public bodies.

The French system of administrative courts is headed by the *Conseil d'Etat*, which acts as both an advisory and a judicial body. The 1958 constitution specified a range of issues on which the government must consult this court before taking action. Below this is the *cour administrative d'appel*. This court possesses judicial powers alone and hears appeals from the *tribunal administratif*. The latter operates on a regional level and like the *Conseil d'Etat* is an advisory and judicial body.

Constitutional law

In some countries the courts may be also called upon to adjudicate on disputes arising from the constitution. Typically this involves assessing whether acts passed by the legislature accord with the statement of fundamental law contained in a country's constitution. But it may also scrutinise actions undertaken by the executive branch (such as the executive orders issued by the American president). If the courts decide that such actions are in breach of the constitution they may be declared 'unconstitutional'. This has the effect of overturning them:

they are rendered 'null and void'. Additionally, the courts may be required to determine the constitutionality of actions undertaken by sub-national bodies such as state governments. Such adjudication is frequently required in federal states. The courts may also have to ensure that the allocation of responsibilities within and between the institutions of government remains as was provided for in the constitution.

With the exception of commitments associated with Britain's membership of the European Union, a country such as Britain which lacks a codified constitution does not have any process whereby the actions of bodies such as Parliament can be overturned. Such a procedure would be contrary to the concept of the sovereignty of Parliament. This doctrine insists that Parliament is the sole source of law-making power whose actions cannot be overruled by any other body. However, countries with codified constitutions frequently have a procedure whereby a court may scrutinise the actions undertaken by the legislature, executive or other tiers of government. This process is termed judicial review. The manner whereby this process is performed and the tasks which it involves vary greatly from one country to another.

In America the process of judicial review is performed by the supreme court. This consists of nine judges appointed by the president subject to the consent of the Senate. Their intervention occurs when cases are referred to them on appeal either from the highest courts of appeal in the states or from the federal court of appeal. This body's interpretation of the constitution was influential in establishing the civil rights of black Americans during the 1950s and 1960s.

THE FRENCH CONSTITUTIONAL COURT

In France the *Conseil Constitutionnel* is responsible for ensuring that the constitution is adhered to. This body was instituted in the 1958 constitution. It consists of nine members who are not required to be legally trained judges. Three of these are appointed by the president of France, three by the president of the National Assembly and three by the president of the Senate. They serve for nine years and may not be renominated. Former presidents of the republic may also serve on this body.

Unlike the American supreme court, there are some limitations placed on the jurisdiction of this body and it further exercises a range of advisory powers (including the requirement that it has to be consulted if the president intends to exercise emergency powers).

In Germany the federal constitutional court ensures that the constitution is obeyed. This body was established in 1951 and it is staffed by a mixture of career judges and nominees drawn from a range of groups including political parties. These are formally appointed by the *Bundesrat* and *Bundestag*. In addition to its ability to declare law unconstitutional it has further involved itself in the process of law making by suggesting how a law which it has declared to be unconstitutional can be amended in order to comply with the constitution.

In Italy the task of upholding the constitution is shared between a constitutional court and the president of the Republic. The former's role includes acting as a court of impeachment for the president, prime minister and other ministers. The latter's tasks include ensuring that the actions of the executive and legislature conform to the relationship specified in the constitution.

Judicial interpretation

In what sense can it be argued that judges are law makers?

In theory the role of judges is to apply the law or the constitution to the matter which comes before them. However, it is often argued that judges go beyond this role and effectively determine its contents which are subsequently binding on courts dealing with similar cases. This situation arises as a result of judicial interpretation of such documents which may effectively give judges the ability to act in a law-making capacity. They differ, however, in the principles which may be applied when interpreting the law or constitution.

The strict letter of the law

Some judges rigidly apply the wording of the statute or constitution to the case in hand. The judge's interpretation, therefore, is little more than the citation of existing sources as the basis for the decision which is reached. A case is determined according to the strict letter of the law. This strict interpretation view of the role of the judiciary tends to promote a conservative approach to judicial interpretation. It suggests that issues which are not contained in a country's law or constitution cannot be inserted into it by judges. Those who subscribe to such a view regard this as either the work of legislators or as a matter which should be responded to by the process of constitutional amendment.

Judicial activism

Other judges, however, exercise a wider degree of discretion when interpreting the law or constitution. Some who are faced with a situation which is not strictly covered by existing law or constitutional provision, may believe it to be their responsibility to bring the existing law or the constitution up to date. Alternatively, a statute or constitutional provision at issue in a case may lack precision or be ambiguous and thus capable of having more than one meaning. The judge will thus be required to give an opinion as to the correct course of action which should be pursued. In these situations judicial interpretation departs from the precise wording of the law or constitution. It may be guided by one or other of two principles.

Judges may decide a case according to the spirit of the law or constitution. That is, they reach a verdict based upon what is viewed to be compatible with existing law or constitutional enactments rather than what is actually contained in them. In reaching their judgment, judges may seek to determine what was in the minds of those who initially drafted the law or constitution and apply this to the case before them. Other judges may go beyond this. They may consider it their duty to adjudicate a case according to what they believe should be contained in the law or constitution rather than what actually is there.

These two latter situations enable a judge to advance beyond the mere administration of the law and, instead, to act in the capacity of a legislator. That is, they advance existing law or create new law through the ability they give themselves to interpret laws and constitutions. The term 'judicial activism' is applied to the situation in which judges exercise a positive role in policy making.

Judicial interpretation may help to ensure that the law or constitution is kept up to date or accords with changing public sentiments as to what constitutes reasonable conduct. However, critics of this role argue that judges ought to distinguish between interpreting the law and actually writing it. They assert that judicial interpretation leads judges to perform a role which ought to be carried out by the legislative branch of government or through the process of constitutional amendment.

The politics of the judiciary

To what extent is the operations of the judiciary subject to political considerations?

The above discussion has suggested that judges often perform the role of policy makers. Here we consider the political environment within which judges operate and the effect which this has on all aspects of their work. We know from our own experiences that it is difficult to act in a totally detached and neutral manner. Our actions are likely to be based upon our personal values. Judges are no exception to this. Below we evaluate some of the factors which might influence the way in which judges discharge their responsibilities and the extent to which they are sufficiently accountable for their actions.

Personal values

Some actions might be flavoured by the personal values of the judge. These may stem from the judge's social background or legal training. This suggests that it is desirable that judges should be representative of the society in which they operate in terms such as class, gender or race. If judges are socially unrepresentative they may be open to the accusation of discriminatory conduct towards those from a different background.

Political opinions

The political opinions held by a judge may also influence how that official operates. These may derive from the position which the judiciary operates in the machinery of the state. In a liberal democracy judges may regard the preservation of this system of government to be of paramount importance. This may influence the attitude which judges display in cases when state interests are involved.

Alternatively, these opinions may consist of the judge's own political preferences. In America presidents often seek to promote their political values through the appointments which they make to the federal judicial system, especially to the supreme court. They thus appoint judges to these positions whose political views mirror their own.

THE POLITICS OF JUDICIAL APPOINTMENT IN AMERICA

In America all federal judges and justices of the supreme court are appointed by the president. Enquiries into a candidate's background are initiated on behalf of the chief executive. Following this, however, they are required to be confirmed by the Senate whose Judiciary Committee conducts hearings into a nominee's suitability. Judges of the supreme court serve for life subject to 'good behaviour'. The ability of this body to over-rule state and federal legislators and the chief executive influences presidents to appoint judges whose political views closely correspond to their own. For similar reasons, the Senate may pay regard to issues other than the professional competence of a nominee when he or she comes before them for confirmation.

Some presidents have the opportunity to appoint a large number of federal judges, and others very few. However, when one party has filled the office of president for a number of years, it is likely that the composition of the federal courts will reflect this control. Thus when President Clinton entered office in 1992 he was faced with a conservative supreme court whose personnel had been mainly chosen by previous Republican presidents. Decisions related to affirmative action and the desegregation of schools announced in 1995 illustrated the political significance of this situation.

Judicial accountability

We have suggested that the personal views of judges and political considerations might influence the way in which the courts operate. If we accept that judges are able to inject personal or political biases into their work, especially when interpreting the law or constitution, we need to examine the sufficiency of mechanisms through which judges can be made to explain and justify their actions and, if necessary, be punished for them. In a liberal democracy members of the legislative and executive branches of government (who in theory are charged with initiating and carrying out legislation) are accountable for their actions. Ultimately they rely on public support to enter or remain in public office. Judges, however, are usually insulated from any direct form of political accountability for their actions, even when these have a fundamental bearing on political affairs. They are usually unelected (although this method of appointment does apply in some American states) and once appointed enjoy security of tenure.

There are, however, some formal controls over the activities of judges. These include the ability of politicians to intervene in the operations of the criminal justice system and the use of juries which may help to offset judicial biases. The decisions of judges can also be set aside by a revision to the law or an amendment to the constitution.

THE TENURE OF JUDGES

Liberal democratic political systems usually give judges considerable security of tenure. This is designed to ensure that these public officials cannot be placed under pressure to determine cases according to the wishes of the government of the day.

In Britain, for example, senior judges can only be removed by an address of both Houses of Parliament to the Queen. In Ireland judges can only be dismissed for misbehaviour and incapacity and to do this requires resolutions from the *Dáil* and the *Seanad*. Additionally, an Irish judge's remuneration may not be reduced during that official's continuance in office.

This situation tends to make judges insufficiently accountable for their actions. Judges are able to say and do more or less what they like in the sure knowledge that they do not have to answer directly to politicians or to the public at large. This is particularly a problem when judicial interpretation effectively gives judges a key role in the determination of public policy.

Additionally, judges may be subject to informal pressures. In particular they may be influenced by a consideration of what is acceptable to the public at large and seek to ensure that their judgments accord with what they discern as the prevailing political consensus. It has been argued that the American supreme court watches the election returns. This is of particular importance when the courts are required to determine a politically emotive issue. This suggests that public and political opinion may play a role in determining judicial decisions. Courts possess authority rather than power. Compliance to their decisions (for example by lower level courts or by public officials) is thus more likely when these are supported by a degree of political or public approval. But it may not always be a straightforward matter to operate in this fashion. Contentious issues will divide the public and make it impossible for the judiciary to avoid political controversy.

Questions

1 Consider the advantages and disadvantages which arise from the control over police forces being exclusively exercised by:
   (a) national government
   (b) local government
   (c) senior police officers.
2 What do you understand by the process of 'judicial review'? Illustrate the operations of this process in any country with which you are familiar.
3 'Much of the work performed by judges involves them in policy-making':
   • Why does this situation arise?
   • Are there any dangers associated with it?
4 Do you believe it is desirable to make judges more politically accountable for their actions?

Summary

1 The police and courts operate in a political environment which shapes their role and activities.
2 The control and accountability of the police is subject to a wide variety of different mechanisms in liberal democratic political structures. National government, local government and the police themselves may each play a role in these processes.
3 A divided system of control over policing exists in Britain in which the Home Office, chief constables and a local police authority share

responsibilities for this public service. This makes for what is known as a 'tripartite system of accountability' which has not operated efficiently since it was formally introduced in 1964.

4 The structure and organisation of judicial systems is subject to variation within liberal democracies. In most countries a basic division exists between civil and criminal law and some also possess a separate system of administrative law. Countries with a written constitution accord the judiciary the responsibility of determining whether a law or action undertaken by the executive is in accordance with the constitution and gives the judiciary the power to set aside measures which in their view are 'unconstitutional'.

5 The ability of judges to interpret either the law or a constitution may result in them performing a law-making role. This may arise when judges determine cases which come before them in accordance with the spirit of such enactments or what they believe these should contain rather than their precise or actual wordings.

6 It is difficult for a judge to be free from personal or political biases and these may affect the way in which this official functions. Although judges may be subject to some formal and informal constraints, they are mainly free from mechanisms to provide for an effective means of accountability for their actions.

12

SUB-NATIONAL
GOVERNMENT

Definition

What is meant by the term 'sub-national government'?

A major role performed by government is to provide services for the benefit of the general public. Many of these are provided by national government. However, others are controlled and administered by bodies covering only part of a particular country. There are a wide variety of these, but in this chapter we will confine our attention to state, regional and local authorities. These constitute important examples of what is meant by 'sub-national government'.

Sub-national governments are subject to considerable variation. A key distinction concerns the autonomy which such units enjoy. In federal states such as Germany, Australia or America, power is divided between the national (or federal) government and the constituent states. The division of responsibilities is provided for in a single source, usually a written constitution, which allocates specific functions to each sphere of government. Each enjoys autonomy in its own area of jurisdiction which means that one may not intrude into the operations of the other. There may also be functions which are exercised jointly by both tiers of government.

CONFEDERATION

A confederate system of government is one in which the national government has extremely limited powers relative to

---

the responsibilities of state governments, thus making for a weak central authority. A particular feature of a confederation is that the national government has no direct powers over citizens: functions such as taxation and law enforcement are exercised by the constituent governments.

A confederate system of government lacking an effective executive branch existed in America between 1781 and 1788. The Southern States which seceded in the Civil War were also subject to this form of government between 1861 and 1865. The Commonwealth of Independent States (which was established following the collapse of the Soviet Union) is a recent creation.

The alternative to a federal state is a unitary one. In unitary states political power is centralised in the hands of the national government. Countries which include Britain, Sweden and France possess such forms of government. However, unitary states often possess a unit of government which is intermediate between national and local government. These are usually regional bodies which provide services for a relatively wide geographic area whose inhabitants share some form of common identity such as language, culture or race. Regional authorities vary according to the autonomy which they possess: some exercise power which is devolved from national government thus giving them a wide degree of control over such delegated responsibilities while others merely function as administrative bodies whose role is to provide regional services according to guidelines laid down by national government.

In both federal and unitary states a range of services are provided by subordinate authorities, termed 'local government'. The scope of their activities and extent of their autonomy is subject to wide variation. In many Western European and Scandinavian countries and in America, local government is created by constitutional enactment and has the ability to perform any function unless expressly forbidden to do so by law. This is termed 'general competence'. In Britain and Ireland, however, local government has no constitutional status. Its existence is derived from legislation and it may only perform those functions which are expressly allocated to it by legislation. This situation tends to drastically curtail the autonomy which is exercised by local authorities in these two countries, although in Britain discretionary powers

provide such bodies with a significant degree of operational and inno-
vatory freedom.

Federalism

*What are the strengths and weaknesses of a federal system of govern-
ment?*

Advantages

We have identified the division of power between a national government and constituent units such as states or provinces as the essence
of a federal form of government. This situation possesses a number of
advantages which are discussed below.

An aid to the relationship between the government and its citizens
Federalism was historically viewed as a safeguard against the overbearing power of a strong, central government. In large countries it
breaks down the remoteness which would otherwise occur if government were provided by a distant national authority. Government is
thus brought closer to the people who additionally are provided with
the means to participate in its activities through the process of voting
or through their involvement with locally-orientated pressure groups.

Facilitating diversity in one country
New Right ideology emphasises the virtues which derive from the
diversity with which a federal system of government may be associated.
Variations within one country in matters such as taxation or the level
of services may prove attractive to citizens or to commercial organisations who are encouraged to move from part of the country to another
to benefit themselves. Diversity may thus encourage competition
between states to attract people and industry.

Maintenance of national unity
The autonomy possessed by state governments in a federal system
may be of benefit to nations whose existence is threatened by significant internal division. Provided that a nation provides recognisable
political or economic benefits to all of its citizens, groups with diver-
gent interests may be encouraged to remain within the one state
when the power possessed by the national government is limited with
most functions being provided by governments controlled by local people. Federalism thus empowers localities to run most aspects of their

affairs in accordance with the wishes of the people who reside there with restricted 'interference' by a national government. It may thus contribute towards retaining the existence of states threatened by separatist tendencies. Belgium granted considerable powers of self-government to its Flemish and Walloon communities within the confines of a federation in order to prevent the break-up of the state along linguistic lines. For similar reasons a wide degree of autonomy has been granted to the Canadian province of Quebec.

FEDERALISM IN CANADA

Canada consists of a federation of provinces. There exist strong separatist forces in one of these, Quebec. This is under-laid by its French language and culture.

In an attempt to retain national unity, Canada's federal system of government has provided Quebec with considerable powers of self-government especially in connection with the official use of French. However, this situation has not been to the satisfac-tion of many 'Québecois' who desire separation. This would enable Quebec to negotiate future relations with the remainder of Canada on its own terms. In 1995 a referendum was held on the issue of separation. The people of Quebec rejected it by the narrowest of margins.

The existing level of self-government contributed to the rejec-tion of separation: the continued unity of the nation will depend on the national government re-defining its relations with Quebec through the provision of a special status which will provide an enhanced degree of autonomy within a federal structure of government.

Disadvantages

Fragmentation of government
Government is fragmented, diverse standards of service provision operating in a single country are not necessarily desirable and a minority may be given the means to frustrate the will of the majority. The progress of civil rights in America has been impeded by the ability of Southern State governments to resist or to slow down the imple-mentation of such legislation. Some of these problems may, however,

be mitigated. In America, for example, the existence of intergovernmental bureaucracies, composed of paid officials operating at all levels of government, has served to promote common approaches to problems which all tiers of government pursue.

Enhancement of the power of national governments
A particular difficulty with federalism concerns the distribution of power between the national and constituent governments. This division is provided for in the constitution, and disputes between the two tiers of government are arbitrated by a constitutional court. However, a tendency for the power of national governments to be enhanced at the expense of states has been observed in many federal countries. In America this alteration to the fundamental nature of federalism has partly arisen from judicial interpretation of the constitution in a manner which is favourable towards national governments playing an increased role in economic and social policies. A particular consequence has been increased reliance by the states on revenue provided by national government. This has made for a style of government in which collaboration between the two tiers (and especially by their public officials) has become essential.

FEDERALISM IN AMERICA

America pioneered the federal system of government. Its history suggests that federalism is not a fixed form of government but is fluid and adaptable to changed political and economic circumstances. It has progressed through the following stages:

- *Dual federalism*: this emphasised central and state governments exercising sovereignty in their own spheres of activity. This view was based upon the Tenth Amendment to the Constitution which reserved to the states all powers not specifically delegated to the federal government in the constitution.

- *Co-operative federalism*: this emerged after 1933 when states were required to act in a partnership with the national government and implement programmes to alleviate the effects of the Depression for which they received financial aid. The grant in aid provided by the federal government was the main mechanism to secure such co-ordinated action.

The role of local government as a third partner in solving problems of national importance was especially enhanced by President Johnson's Creative Federalism and the New Federalism of Presidents Nixon and Ford. President Reagan's attempts to make the states more financially self-reliant was dubbed 'fend for yourself federalism'. He also viewed the states as mechanisms to further the federal government's policies.

Financial aid to state governments may erode the independence of the latter. This became a particular issue in Germany following unification since the states which comprised the former country of East Germany were heavily dependent on federal financial support. Such money may be given to states largely to use as they please (as occurs in Germany and was the case with President Nixon's General Revenue Sharing policy in America) or it may be attached to stringent conditions which states have to meet (as occurred under President Reagan). The states' freedom of action may also be circumscribed by action imposed by the national government, designed to enforce conformity and set minimum standards of service provision. In America, pre-emption is an example of the latter. This imposes a legal requirement on states to meet certain minimum standards or to provide stipulated services.

Nonetheless, states continue to play an important role in the economic and social life of a federal country. In America, for example, the ability of the states to raise some of their own revenue and their role as implementors of public policy may enhance their image as dynamic institutions even if they are subject to strong central control exerted by the federal government over many aspects of their operations.

Regionalism

What functions are served by regional machinery of government?

States with unitary systems of government are often accused of being centralised: power resides in the capital and citizens living in areas which are geographically distant from this area may feel neglected by a government which they regard as remote. Some unitary states, therefore, have utilised regional apparatus to offset the disadvantages which are sometimes perceived in a centralised state. This involves a state being divided into a number of smaller areas within which certain tasks of government can be discharged. The role and composition of regional machinery is variable and many different forms may be used even in one state. We consider the main varieties of regional machinery below.

Advisory

Regional machinery may be purely advisory. It can be utilised as a consultative mechanism to facilitate overall government planning or it might be established by individual government departments to aid the flow of information between that department and citizens living in each region. This may enable central government to adjust the operations of a policy to suit the particular requirements of a region and its inhabitants or it may be used to provide advice on government policies to people or public authorities residing there. Such machinery typically includes civil servants and possesses no power other than the ability to act as a vehicle which facilitates a two-way process of communication between government and the governed.

Administrative and governmental

A region may alternatively provide the geographic unit around which services are administered. This embraces the decentralised regional apparatus used by national governmental organisations but also includes regional machinery which has been established to provide services. Regional machinery may be established to discharge individual services: in Ireland, for example, health services have been provided by Area Health Boards since 1971. Alternatively several governmental functions can be co-ordinated at a regional level. In the United Kingdom, the Scottish and Welsh Offices are responsible for a range of services in these two countries which are performed by individual government departments in England. Those who administer services in this fashion may possess some discretion to tailor them to address specific regional needs or requirements.

Regional machinery may be given some degree of power. This will often be exercised by representatives who are elected at regional level and then discharge a range of services over which they possess partial or total control. In Italy and France regional bodies established since 1970 have exercised control over a wide range of functions.

DEVOLUTION, FEDERALISM AND HOME RULE

- *Devolution* involves the transfer of power from a superior to an inferior political authority. The dominance of the former is generally exhibited through its ability to reform or take away the power which it has bestowed.

- *Federalism* necessitates a division of power between central and sub-national governments. The existence of the latter and the general range of powers they possess is usually embodied in a constitution.

- *Home rule* requires the break-up of a nation into a number of sovereign states each exercising total control over their internal and external affairs. This demand is usually based on the existence of a national identity.

The role of local government

What advantages does local government bring to the operations of liberal democratic forms of government?

Local government has responsibility for the administration of a range of services to people living in a relatively small geographic area. Many of the functions traditionally associated with local government constitute services which are utilised by large numbers of citizens on a daily basis. These include the provision of housing, social services, environmental services, refuse disposal and planning. Education is frequently provided by local government, although in France this service has traditionally been subject to a considerable degree of central control. Below we consider the major advantages which local government may bring to the operations of the liberal democratic state.

Local accountability

A major advantage stems from the fact that local government is composed of elected officials. In English-speaking liberal democracies these are usually termed 'councillors'. They can be held accountable to the local electorate for the way in which services are provided. In this way the functions discharged by government can be aligned with what local people desire. There are alternative ways to provide services (such as through development corporations which have been used selectively in Britain since 1979) but the elected dimension of local government is the key to its responsiveness to local issues and problems.

Efficiency in service provision

It has been further suggested that local government is the most efficient way to provide public services. Its size enables local (and often untypical) problems to be addressed which might be overlooked were all government services administered by larger geographic units such as state or regional governments. Local government is also flexible in its approach to problems and has the ability to innovate in an attempt to find solutions to them. In Britain equal opportunity policies were pioneered by local authorities during the 1980s.

Advocacy of minority interests

Local government may also help to overcome the problem of marginalisation. Minority groups within society may be encouraged to become involved in conventional political activity at local level as it presents a realistic possibility that some of their problems might be redressed. In both Britain and America a significant number of councillors derive from ethnic minority backgrounds. This involvement may reduce the likelihood of minority groups having to resort to more extreme forms of political activity which have a damaging effect on social harmony.

Participation

The existence of local government enhances the ability of citizens to participate in the administration of their own affairs. They may do this by voting in local government elections or by serving as elected members of local authorities. Local government thus increases the number of persons in a state able to take decisions related to the administration of its affairs.

Linking citizens with national government

In many countries local government is viewed as a training ground for politicians who later occupy high national office. In Britain, Prime Minister John Major commenced his political career as a councillor in Lambeth, London.

Local government may also further serve as an institutional mechanism which links local people with national government. This is especially apparent in France where leading politicians sometimes hold elected office in municipal government. Jacques Chirac, for example, held the powerful position of Mayor of Paris between 1977 and 1995. This situation also provides national politicians with powerful localised bases of support.

Acting as a pressure group

A final important role performed by local government is its ability to act as a pressure group, putting forward local needs or concerns to other tiers of government and seeking remedies, perhaps through the provision of increased funds to the locality or by changes in central government policy. The early 1980s witnessed some Labour-controlled local authorities providing confrontational opposition to Conservative government policies which they believed were harmful to local people. The ability of local government to act in this manner is enhanced by its elected base which implies it is acting at the behest of local majority opinion.

BAROMETERS OF PUBLIC OPINION

The role of local government goes beyond the provision of services. Local government elections may also provide evidence of the political mood of the nation and serve as a means whereby the general public can exert influence over the conduct or composition of the national government.

The good performance of the Popular Party and the poor showing of the Socialists in Spain's 1995 municipal elections was one pressure exerted on the Socialist prime minister, Felipe González to call an early general election in 1996 in which he was narrowly defeated.

The performance of local government

However, the benefits which are meant to derive from the operations of local government are not always fully realised. Local government may be unable to respond effectively to current issues. Its organisational base may be inappropriate and its revenue-generating capacity inadequate to offer workable solutions to problems such as urban poverty which are manifested at local level, especially in inner city areas. In such places the demand for services is high but the ability of people to pay for them is low. This tends to drive up the level of local taxes and encourage wealthier people to move away. This scenario may result in increased reliance on finance supplied by state or national governments or lead to the delivery of services by purpose-built bodies detached from the organisational structure of local government.

The receptiveness of local government to local needs and problems is also subject to challenge. This may be diminished by the working practices adopted by local government officers or by the concentration of political power within local government. Services are administered by full-time officers who may put their professional interests above the requirements of their clients. In Britain developments such as corporate management which were designed to provide services in a more efficient manner tended to centralise political power within a local authority making it seem remote and distant to ordinary people. The decentralisation of locally administered services is one solution to this problem but it has not been pursued in Britain with the vigour found in other European countries such as France and Spain.

Perhaps as a result of the above two deficiencies, public interest in local government may be low in some countries. In Britain, for example, the turnout in local elections rarely rises above 40%. This suggests that here local government is not particularly effective as a vehicle through which people can participate in the process of government.

Further, in most liberal democracies, local elections are contested by the national political parties. This means that the outcome of local election contests is greatly influenced by national political issues: factors such as the degree of popular support for the national government may be more influential in determining the outcome of a local election than the performance of the authority and the personnel in control of it.

Local autonomy

In what ways are the operations of local government subject to control by the machinery of national government?

In most liberal democracies, local government is subject to a considerable degree of control by national or state governments. This may be exercised in a number of ways which are discussed below.

Miscellaneous control by the executive branch

The executive branch may impose a range of controls on the operations of local government. These include specific controls over individual services, limits on local government spending or detailed controls over local government borrowing. In Ireland central supervision is also exerted over the personnel employed by local authorities.

The prefectoral system

A further way in which local government can be controlled by higher political authorities is through the prefectoral system. This involves the imposition of an official appointed by central government to act as its eyes and ears in the localities and to provide a link between central and local government, effectively fusing the two levels of administration.

In France the prefect (who was termed 'Commissioner of the Republic' between 1982 and 1987) is a civil servant appointed by the Ministry of the Interior and placed in each *departement* and, after 1972, in each region. The prefect formerly exerted considerable day-to-day powers over the *departements* and their constituent local government units (termed 'Communes'). The extent of such power over local authority actions was subject to variation but was universally reduced by reforms enacted by the Socialist government in the 1980s. These served to reduce the previously highly centralised nature of French local government. However, prefects continue to wield supervisory powers over local government. The importance of this might be displayed should any of the three cities controlled by the *Front national* following the 1995 municipal elections seek to implement their 'national preference' policy. If this occurred the prefects might intervene to ensure that equality and anti-discrimination provisions in French law were upheld.

In Italy the prefect also serves as a state representative in the localities (termed 'provinces'). This official is usually an official of the Ministry of the Interior, but is sometimes a career politician. In theory the prefect's main role is to co-ordinate the work of central government ministries at local level although in practice much attention is directed at the maintenance of public order and security.

Judicial control

In countries in which the powers of local government are rigidly controlled by legislation, judicial control may constitute an important control. In Britain, for example, the courts are able to intervene and prevent local authorities from performing functions which they are not legally empowered to perform (and, possibly, to surcharge the councillors who authorised such 'illegal' expenditure) and may also force a council to discharge its mandatory duties if it was ignoring these.

LOCAL GOVERNMENT OR ADMINISTRATION?

There is an important difference between the terms 'government' and 'administration' when applied to local government. The former implies a degree of discretion, usually guaranteed by the fact that local government raises a proportion of its own revenue by taxing its inhabitants.

The latter term suggests that local government has no independence of action and exists to provide services whose content is structured by national or state governments. It is effectively an agent of central government. The extent of local autonomy may be one factor which influences popular involvement in the affairs of local government.

Local government reform in Britain

What innovations have been introduced by Conservative governments since 1979 in central–local government relationships?

Conservative governments have displayed a critical attitude towards local government since 1979. Local authorities have been accused of waste and inefficiency exacerbated by poor management, and of putting political interests before service to the community. This has resulted in increased central control being exerted over them and a loss of functions which they have traditionally performed.

Reform to the structure of local government

The structure of local government has been subject to alteration. The two-tier system of county and district councils which was implemented under the provisions of the 1972 Local Government Act was abandoned in the major urban areas in 1986 when the Greater London Council and the Metropolitan County Councils were abolished. There has latterly been a move towards the establishment of single-tier, or unitary authorities, throughout Wales, Scotland and much of Britain on the grounds that it is more efficient and cost-effective for services to be administered by one set of hands.

Loss of functions

Services have also been taken out of the hands of local government and transferred to a range of alternative authorities including joint boards, quangos and central government. The involvement of central government has greatly increased in policy areas such as education which was traditionally viewed as a local responsibility. Government policy has also served to weaken the role performed by local government in functions which include the provision of public housing. At the behest of government policy initiated in the 1980 Housing Act, one million council houses have been sold and much of the work previously carried out by local authorities in this area has been assumed by housing associations.

Controls over local government spending

Additional controls have been introduced designed to curtail the level of expenditure by local government. This has been justified by the argument that the national government is required to exercise overall control over the level of public spending. Such legislation has included the 1980 Local Government, Planning and Land Act, the 1982 Local Government Finance Act and the 1984 Rates Act.

Estimates of what each local authority needed to spend were drawn up by central government initially in the form of 'grant related expenditure'. This determined the level of local government grant paid to local authorities by central government, but it was possible to exceed the government's overall estimate by raising additional funds locally through the rates. Accordingly 'capping' was introduced in 1984, which allowed the government to enforce a ceiling on the overall expenditure of those authorities who were viewed as particularly spendthrift. In 1990 Standing Spending Assessments were introduced which were designed to influence the level of locally raised revenue.

Like the previous grant related expenditure, these limits were also underlaid by the sanction of capping.

The key reform introduced by the Conservative Party which sought to curb local government spending was the introduction of a new source of finance through which local governments would fund their operations. The rates (which were taxes levied on property) were replaced by a tax on individuals. This was the Community Charge, more infamously known as 'poll tax'. It was designed to enhance the accountability of local government to its residents by forcing all citizens to contribute towards the costs of local government. It this way it was envisaged that high spending councils would be more readily sanctioned by local electors since exemptions and rebates associated with the rating system resulted in a significant number of local residents having to make no financial contribution to the costs of local services. This new tax became law in 1988 and was first introduced in England and Wales in 1990.

However, the introduction of poll tax was surrounded by controversy. It was an extremely difficult and expensive tax to collect and the problems were compounded by a campaign seeking to encourage people not to pay. It was argued that the tax was essentially unfair by making all contribute regardless of their means. Eventually the government was forced to back down. Poll tax was abandoned and replaced by the Council Tax as local government's independent source of finance. This was essentially a tax on property, the level of which was determined by the value of property (which was viewed as suggestive of the financial means of its occupants). In 1990 a Uniform Business Rate was introduced to govern the financial contribution made by business concerns towards the costs of local authorities in which they are situated.

Conservative reforms to local government finance have served to enhance the power of central government over the level of local spending.

Privatisation

The concept of market forces has also been introduced into local government. A large number of operations have been transferred from direct local government control and made subject to competitive tendering. Legislation which includes the 1980 Local Government,

Planning and Land Act and the 1988 and 1990 Local Government Acts have moved local government in the direction of an enabling authority rather than one which directly provides services. The implication that people may be attracted to move to the most efficient and cost-effective local authorities has been enhanced by the Audit Commission's publication, commencing in 1995, of local authority performance indicators. The Conservative government has also sought to involve the private sector in projects which include the rejuvenation of declining urban areas. Although this may involve local government working in partnership with financial and business interests this approach has, on occasions, resulted in the establishment of bodies such as urban development corporations and task forces which have bypassed local government.

INTERNAL CONTROL OF LOCAL GOVERNMENT

This is subject to wide variation between and within liberal democratic systems of government. There are, however, certain key considerations.

The executive arm of local government is varied. A key distinction exists between a directly-elected executive (such as the American mayor) or an executive selected from the leading members of the largest political party represented on the local authority. The latter is the case in Britain, although one person, termed the 'leader of the council' often wields considerable control over local authority affairs.

Internal management is also subject to variation. Ireland utilises the council manager system in which all services are co-ordinated by one person. The manager's position and powers are based on legislation. In Britain the office of chief executive has not fully eroded the power exercised by individual local government committees.

Questions

1 List the key differences which distinguish a unitary system of government from a federal one. Provide two examples of each.
2 'Local government performs an indispensable role in the operations of liberal democratic systems of government.' What main arguments would you put forward to support this assertion?
3 On the basis of your knowledge of the operations of central–local government relationships in liberal democracies, provide five examples of the manner in which central government control may be exerted over local government.
4 With reference to any country with which you are familiar, present a brief summary (including the use of a diagram) of the structure of sub-national government which is found there.

Summary

1 The study of government is not confined to national government but extends to an investigation of the role served by units which operate at a sub-national level. These include state and local governments and regional units of administration.
2 In a federal system of government, power is shared between a national government and constituent units such as states. This division is sanctioned in a written constitution. Federalism may provide diversity in the provision of services and may also give a sufficient level of self-government to the states which serves to preserve the existence of nations which are divided on racial or cultural lines. However, federalism may result in diverse standards of service provision in one country or make it possible for localised minority opinions to frustrate the will of the national majority. Federalism is a fluid system of government whose nature has been considerably influenced by the reliance of con-stituent units on finances provided by central government.
3 The regional machinery of government utilised by liberal democratic states is subject to wide variation: it ranges from being purely advisory to governmental.
4 Local government brings a number of advantages to liberal democratic states. These include:
   • delivery of services in a manner which is responsive to local needs.

- provision of a mechanism through which citizens can participate in running their own affairs and which may link people and national government.
- alerting central government to the needs of particular localities through local government's ability to act as a consumer pressure group.

5   However, there are problems associated with the operations of local government. These include:
- its structure and financial resources may be inadequate to solve contemporary issues, especially associated with urban poverty.
- local government is sometimes accused of being remote from its residents.

6   There are a wide variety of means whereby central government can exert control over local government. These include controls over spending, borrowing and the performance of individual services. In France, officials of central government (the prefects) are placed within the localities to supervise the activities of local government. In Britain, the period since 1979 has witnessed a considerable erosion of the role and autonomy of local government. Key reforms have included the imposition of limits on local government spending and the loss in many areas of activity, of local government's ability to act as direct service providers.

13

THE NATION-STATE IN THE MODERN WORLD

The concept

What does the term 'sovereignty' mean?

Sovereignty implies self-determination. The term suggests that a state has the ability to control its own affairs without interference from outside bodies and countries. In particular sovereignty suggests that a state has the exclusive right to pass laws which administer that nation's affairs.

As we have seen in Chapter 12, sovereignty is shared within federal states. In countries which include America, Australia, Canada and Germany, the national government may enact legislation in certain areas of activity and other matters are subject to regulation by states or provinces which comprise these countries. The division of power is provided for in a codified constitution and a constitutional court arbitrates when problems arise as to whether a particular function should be regulated by national or sub-national governments. In unitary countries such as Britain and France, sovereignty is not divided. Power resides in central government which theoretically has the sole and unlimited right to regulate the affairs of these nations.

THE BRITISH CONCEPT OF THE SOVEREIGNTY OF PARLIAMENT

The sovereignty of Parliament is at the heart of Britain's system of government. It implies that Parliament may pass any legislation which it wishes whose implementation cannot then be challenged by any other body within the state (such as a court or a local authority). Initially this doctrine was designed to provide for the pre-eminence of Parliament over the monarchy.

The concept of the sovereignty of Parliament also suggests that one Parliament cannot bind a successor to a course of action. Any law passed by one Parliament can be subsequently amended or repealed. This includes legislation securing British membership to supranational bodies such as the European Union.

Threats to sovereignty

Does sovereignty remain a viable concept in the late twentieth century?

It is doubtful whether any state has ever enjoyed total control over the conduct of its affairs. The nineteenth century nation-state perhaps went some way to approximating this ideal, but such countries were often required to pay regard to outside factors affecting their internal or external activities. In the twentieth century sovereignty is even less of a reality: the ability of any state to function autonomously has been limited by a wide range of factors.

Supranational governmental institutions

Many countries affiliate to governmental organisations which operate across national boundaries. The European Union is an example of such a body. Membership of supranational institutions places limitations on the activities of the member countries whose sovereignty is thus restricted by the expectation that they will adhere to the policies determined by the central decision-making machinery of the organisation. The refusal of any member country to do so may result in the deployment of sanctions against it.

Bodies which facilitate intergovernmental co-operation

In addition to supranational organisations which exercise governmental powers across national boundaries, other international bodies primarily serve as forums for co-operation, often in limited areas of state activity. Examples include the United Nations, the North Atlantic

Treaty Organization and the Commonwealth. Such organisations may seek to influence the direction of member (and sometimes non-member) countries through the application of moral pressure, sanctions or force. The decision to suspend Nigeria from membership of the Commonwealth in 1995 was designed to pressurise that country's government to introduce improvements to its civil rights policies. Trade embargoes are a further potent sanction which international bodies may use to force a government to change the direction of its politics. They may also utilise military intervention to accomplish their aims. The use of ground troops in Bosnia under the auspices of NATO sought to ensure the successful implementation of the peace agreement following its endorsement by the presidents of Croatia, Bosnia and Serbia.

International trade

International trade has placed restraints on the actions of national governments. Membership of regional trading blocs such as the European Union or wider arrangements such as the General Agreement on Tariffs and Trade, limit the ability of member countries to pursue policies such as tariff protection against other participating nations. Broader agreements have also been made to regulate the world's trading system through international actions which included the Bretton Woods Agreement and the Group of Seven (G-7) summit meetings. Such initiatives impinge upon the control which individual nations exert over economic policies. Such discretion is further reduced by the need to consider the reaction of financial markets to political decisions taken by individual governments.

Multinational companies

Large-scale economic activity is decreasingly confined to the nation from which a company originates. Developments in the means of communication often mean that such bodies will locate their operations in a number of countries. Incentives to do this include immediate access to raw materials and (in the case of firms locating in the Third World) the availability of cheap labour. Such multinational companies (many of which are American or Japanese) possess considerable influence over the operations of the government of the countries in which they invest. In return for providing jobs and revenue derived from taxing their operations, multinational companies may demand concessions from governments as the price for their investment in that country. In extreme circumstances this may involve direct or indirect control over a country's political system to ensure that government policy is compatible with the needs of the company. If these conflict the government may suffer: in Guatemala, for example, President Jacobo Arbenz's quarrels with the American United Fruit Company resulted in his replacement by an American-backed military government in 1954.

AMERICAN INVOLVEMENT IN LATIN AMERICA

The post-war political affairs of countries in Latin America have been heavily influenced by the United States. There are two reasons for this – military and economic.

Latin America is in close proximity to the United States. The spectre of Soviet missiles being sited in Cuba (which had been removed from the American sphere of influence by a revolution headed by Fidel Castro in 1959) almost triggered a nuclear war in 1962. Central America (particularly the Panama Canal zone) is viewed as the jugular vein of the United States which needs to be controlled by governments who are friendly to that country.

Economic considerations have made Latin America attractive to American multinational companies. They require political stability which has often been delivered by governments reliant on American support who can be trusted to safeguard their interests. National revolutions (such as that which occurred in Nicaragua in 1979) are often opposed by America on economic as well as strategic grounds.

Some commentators have observed that the relationship of First and Third World countries is that of dependency. This theory suggests that the role of Third World countries is to serve the economic interests of the industrially advanced nations. This tends to distort the pattern of economic development in such countries so that it becomes geared to the need of the First World and the multinational companies which are located within them. Dependency is buttressed by loans made available to Third World countries by bodies such as the International Monetary Fund. The interest rates charged and the conditions stipulated by the lending body erode the sovereignty of the receiving country in both political and economic affairs and may result in the pursuance of policies which are to the detriment of many of its inhabitants. The need to export agricultural produce to pay the interest on foreign loans may, for example, result in the local population suffering from hunger and starvation.

Foreign aid

Some countries, especially in the developing world, are in receipt of aid. This includes grants, loans or gifts, which may stimulate agricultural and industrial development or be concerned with military purposes. This aid is provided either by individual governments (termed 'bilateral aid') or by international bodies such as the World Bank or the International Monetary Fund (termed 'multilateral aid'). Foreign aid may be awarded subject to conditions which the receiving government is forced to adopt. These may include fundamental alterations in domestic policy. Aid provided by Western liberal democracies, for example, may require improvements in the receiving country's human rights record.

The media

In Chapter 6 we examined technological developments affecting the structure of the mass media. Changes which have included satellite and cable television and the Internet have transformed the media into a global mechanism which transmits across national frontiers. These new forms of communication have made it more difficult for governments to exert legislative control over the dissemination of information to their citizens since it may be transmitted from installations which operate outside their frontiers and which are effectively beyond their supervision or control. In particular the capacity of a government to exercise censorship is considerably limited by the new advances in communication. In response to this situation, the European Community produced a discussion document in 1984 entitled *Television Without Frontiers* which sought to establish a common regulatory framework from broadcasting across Europe. In 1989 member nations signed a Directive designed to facilitate a free market for television broadcasting across national frontiers.

The institutions of the European Union

The European Union constitutes an important example of a supra-national governmental body: how does it operate?

Membership of the European Union involves the member countries relinquishing some control over their own affairs in areas which are encompassed by its treaties. In these spheres of activity decision making becomes a collective exercise. Britain's voice, for example, is articulated by its 87 Members of the European Parliament, two commissioners and one vote in the Council of Ministers. The following section discusses how the work of the European Union is discharged.

The Commission

This body consists of commissioners appointed by the governments of each member state. Each serves for five years. The commissioners appoint a president who has a two-year term of office. The commissioners are allocated specific responsibilities (termed 'portfolios') by the EU president. They are served by a civil service organised into directorates. The Commission performs a number of key tasks connected with the operations of the European Union. These include the initiation of policy through the preparation of proposals for the consideration of the Council of Ministers. It also prepares a draft budget. It exercises executive functions by implementing policy and also carries out supervisory responsibilities.

The Council of Ministers

The Council is composed of ministers of the member states. The Council 'proper' consists of each country's foreign minister, although much of its work is discharged by sub-committees and working groups in which other ministers may participate. The Council is the European Union's law-making body. Legislation approved by the Council becomes part of the national law of member states. It is in this sense that membership of the EU results in a loss of national sovereignty. This has been to some extent safeguarded by the practice of unanimity, effectively giving individual governments the power to veto proposals and thereby preserve national interests. There is, however, a movement towards taking decisions on the basis of qualified majority votes which would erode the single nation veto. One aspect of what is termed the 'fast track' European integration proposals, enunciated by Chancellor Kohl of Germany and President Chirac of France towards the end of 1995, involves expanding the number of decisions which can be made in this manner.

The European Council

This is a forum of the heads of government of the member states. Its existence was formally recognised in the Single European Act. Its main purpose is to discuss issues of overall importance to the European Union and in this capacity has performed a prominent role in the area of foreign affairs.

KEY TREATIES AFFECTING THE EUROPEAN UNION

1957   The Treaty of Rome: this established the European Economic Community (usually referred to as the 'Common Market').

1986   The Single European Act: this sought to remove obstacles to a frontier-free community by providing the legal framework to achieve a single market by 31 December 1992.

1991   The Maastricht Treaty: this aimed to enhance European unity at the expense of national sovereignty in areas which included economic and monetary policy. Common foreign and security policies were proposed together with an extension of responsibilities in areas including social policy. The British government objected to the 'Social Chapter' designed to protect workers' rights. Following ratification the term 'European Union' was adopted.

The European Parliament

This consists of representatives who are directly elected by the citizens of each member country. MEPs serve for a term of five years. For much of its existence the European Parliament was regarded as a 'talking shop' which considered proposals put forward by the Commission but which exercised little power over decisions. However, the Single European Act and the Maastricht Treaty sought to provide it with a more vigorous role. Its new responsibilities included approving appointments to the Commission and president and playing a more significant role in the law-making process. In 1995 it threatened to utilise such powers and pass a vote of censure against the Commission unless it took action to halt French nuclear tests in the South Pacific Ocean. This course of action, if successful, would force the collective resignation of the Commission. The European Parliament makes wide use of committees and it is these bodies which consider the content of proposed European Union law.

The Court of Justice

A key purpose of the Court is to ensure that European Union law is adhered to by member countries. Disputes between member states, between the European Union and member states, between individuals and the European Union or between the institutions of the European Union are resolved by this Court. It has the power to declare unlawful any national law which contravenes European law and also has the power to fine companies who are found to be in breach of such legislation. The Court is staffed by judges and advocates drawn from member countries. They serve for six years. One example of its power over national law was its decision in 1995 that men in Britain should receive free medical prescriptions at the age of 60, rather than 65, to bring them into a position of equality with women.

EUROPEAN LAW-MAKING

European law is delivered in two main forms: regulations (which are immediately embodied into the law of each member country) and directives (which give member countries some flexibility in implementation).

The European Court of Justice rules in the event of disputes arising concerning the adoption of law by or within member countries. A number of national courts (including those of France and Britain) have upheld the view that European law has precedence over national law when these conflict.

Parliaments in member nations have sought to monitor the activities of the EU by setting up specialist committees. These include Ireland's Joint Committee of the *Oireachtas* on

---

Secondary Legislation, the British House of Commons Select Committee on European Legislation and the short-lived (1983–87) German *Europa-Kommission* composed of members drawn from the *Bundestag* and the European Parliament.

Impact on national governmental organisation

Membership of the European Union has had an impact on the organisation of the machinery of member governments. In Britain, for example, a European Secretariat within the Cabinet Office co-ordinates national policy towards the EU and government departments have divisions concerned with the European dimension to their activities.

The transfer of some decision making to the institutions of the European Union has also had significant implications for those who seek to influence the policy-making process. As we observed in Chapter 5, pressure groups are widely engaged in liaison with the Commission and its officials. Local authorities have also been induced to establish representation in Brussels in connection with proposed bids for aid from sources such as the European Regional Development Fund.

The end of sovereignty?

Is sovereignty a meaningful concept of the late twentieth century?

The above sections have documented some of the restrictions imposed on the freedom of action possessed by national governments. But it would be wrong to assert that nations now have no meaningful control over their internal or external affairs. National economies are subject to broad global considerations and restraints. However, individual governments retain the ability to manage their economies, at least in the short term. In many liberal democracies incumbent governments will initiate policies such as taxation cuts or reductions in the rates of interest in order to court popularity with the electorate.

Individual governments may further pursue a course of action regardless of the opinions of other countries. The decision by the French government in 1995 to resume its programme of nuclear weapon testing in the Pacific Ocean provoked widespread opposition from individual countries such as Australia and New Zealand, from international pressure groups such as Greenpeace and from international organisations such as the Commonwealth. Economic pressure in the form of boycotts against French produce, especially wine, was applied. But the French government ignored such pressures and proceeded with this policy.

Sovereignty remains a term which enters into the rhetoric of political debate and influences political behaviour. In Britain, allegations that sovereignty is threatened by the policies of the European Union remains a potent argument which crosses traditional political divisions.

BRITAIN'S EUROSCEPTICS

Premier Thatcher's Bruges speech in 1988 led to the formation of a faction (the Bruges Group) within the Conservative Party to oppose progress in the direction of a federal Europe. There is also an influential tendency, the Eurosceptics, within that party.

Eurosceptics are especially opposed to any further moves towards pooling sovereignty and political integration which they view as the underpinnings of the Single Market Act and the Maastricht Treaty. They oppose the latter treaty's goal of economic and monetary union, do not wish to re-enter the Exchange Rate Mechanism, and criticise the European Court of Justice for enhancing federalism. A number voted against the ratification of the Maastricht Treaty in 1993 even though the government made this an issue of confidence. Eurosceptic support for the candidacy of John Redwood in the 1995 leadership contest was a major explanation for his good showing against the prime minister, John Major. It demonstrates the potency of the political appeal of sovereignty.

Nationalism

Why are demands for national independence frequently made?

Sovereignty is often associated with nationalism. Post-war history contains numerous examples of national identity being employed as the motivating force for independence movements. Such seek the establishment of self-governing states. Nationalism engenders feelings of patriotism and inspired independence movements in African countries directed against European colonial powers. In Latin America it was the main force behind anti-American movements in many countries, including Cuba and Nicaragua. More recently it dominated events in the former country of Yugoslavia in which nationalism was the justification for 'ethnic cleansing'. The desire to establish a self-governing state has considerable influence on the contemporary politics of Canada and Spain. Here national minorities (the Québecois, Catalans and Basques) desire self-government. In Britain the demand for Scottish and Welsh home rule has been vocally expressed since the late 1960s.

Scottish home rule

Scotland has been part of the United Kingdom since the 1707 Act of Union. The assertion that Scotland has a distinct national identity is put forward in support of the demand for total control over domestic and internal affairs. This demand is articulated by the Scottish National Party.

Home rule has frequently been justified by the argument that the Westminster Parliament neglects the special interests and problems faced by the Scots. It was reinforced during the 1970s by the discovery and development of oil around the Scottish coast. The fact that some countries within the European Union have a smaller population than Scotland has further strengthened the SNP position for a independent Scotland within Europe. Since 1979 Scotland's distinct political identity has been displayed by the overwhelming support given to the Labour Party during a period when English politics have been dominated by the Conservatives.

SCOTTISH NATIONALISM – RECENT KEY EVENTS

1973 The Royal Commission on the Constitution reported: it contained recommendations for legislative assemblies to be set up in Scotland and Wales funded by an independent exchequer board. The assemblies would be at liberty to decide how to spend the global sums they were allocated.

1975	A white paper ('Our Changing Democracy: Devolution to Scotland and Wales') proposed elected assemblies for both countries financed by a block grant and whose actions would be subject to veto by the Secretary of State.
1978	The Scotland and Wales Acts were passed: these stipulated that the devolution proposals would be put to a referendum and to be implemented 40% of the electorates in each country would be required to vote 'yes': an abstention was effectively a 'no' vote. The referendums held in 1979 failed to secure this level of support and the proposals were thus abandoned.

Scottish nationalism has posed a dilemma for Britain's major political parties. The Conservative Party, which is pledged to defend the constitutional status quo, has displayed least interest in fundamental constitutional reform although it has occasionally supported some measure of adjustment to the parliamentary committee system which reviews Scottish affairs.

The Liberal Democrats support a federal system of government which would give the Scots a considerable degree of control over the administration of their domestic affairs but with issues such as the economy and defence being determined by a federal parliament.

The problem faced by the Labour Party is that any major concession towards home rule might reduce the number of Scottish Members of Parliament elected to Westminster. A significant reduction would make the election of a Labour government an extremely unlikely occurrence.

The level of support for the Scottish National Party since the 1992 general election has prompted fresh initiatives from the major political parties. The SNP currently proposes the establishment of a Scottish Parliament elected by a mixture of the first-past-the-post system and the additional-member system with an elected chancellor as its presiding officer. This body would govern an independent Scotland and links with England, Wales and Northern Ireland would be retaining through an organisation entitled the 'Association of States of the British Isles'.

Scottish Labour and Liberal Democrats have co-operated since 1989 in the operations of the Scottish Constitutional Convention which recognised the principle that Scots people had the right to determine the structure of their own government. In 1995 these two parties announced proposals under the auspices of the Convention which involved a Scottish Parliament elected for a fixed term by a method which was designed to add an element of proportionality to the first-past-the-post system. This parliament would elect a chief minister and possess limited powers to vary the United Kingdom rate of income tax. It would be responsible for policies which are currently the responsibility of the Scottish Office.

In 1993 the Conservative government's white paper, 'Scotland in the Union', suggested amended provision for the consideration of Scottish affairs at Westminster. In 1995 proposals were announced to increase the powers of Scottish MPs in this area of activity. Scottish bills would normally be referred to the Scottish Grand Committee for their second and third reading stages and ministers would be required to attend meetings of that committee to explain the government's Scottish policies. A special standing committee, meeting in Scotland, would be established. This would listen to evidence related to Scottish legislation undergoing its committee stage. Enhanced powers for Scottish local authorities were also put forward.

Questions

1 Differentiate between the terms 'sovereignty' and 'sovereignty of Parliament'.
2 In Britain, Eurosceptics object to enhanced political integration at the expense of national sovereignty. Compile a brief summary of the way in which the operations of the institutions of the European Union erode national sovereignty.
3 With reference to any country with which you are familiar, list six areas in which its independence of political and economic action is curtailed.
4 'In spite of the erosion of national sovereignty, national identity remains a potent political force in the modern world.' Produce arguments to support this view, drawing examples from at least one event which has occurred in the 1990s.

Summary

1   Sovereignty indicates the ability of a government to make law for a defined geographic area. In federal systems of government, sovereignty is shared between the national government and constituent state or provincial governments but in unitary systems it is exercised solely by central government.

2   There are limitations which prevent any one government from exercising total control over the entire range of its internal and external affairs. Limits to complete national independence of action are exerted by supranational governmental institutions, bodies which facilitate intergovernmental co-operation, international trade (including the power possessed over national governments by multinational business corporations) and foreign aid programmes. Developments affecting the media have also prevented effective national control being exerted over the dissemination of news and information.

3   The European Union provides an important case study whereby the impact of the institutions of a supranational governmental institution on national sovereignty can be evaluated. Eurosceptics have voiced concern that the long-term goal of a federal European state may be realised if national sovereignty is further eroded through enhanced powers being given to EU bodies.

4   Patriotism and nationalism may provide the sentiments upon which demands for national sovereignty are based. Scottish home rule has been used as a case study to illustrate the potency of nationalism in a unitary state and the different policies which have been put forward as a response to this demand.

14

POPULAR SCEPTICISM WITH THE CONDUCT OF POLITICAL AFFAIRS

Loss of power by citizens

Why do citizens often feel that they have lost the ability to exercise meaningful control over their everyday lives?

In recent years numerous criticisms have been expressed with the conduct of politics within a large number of liberal democracies. In many of them citizens felt a loss of power, an inability to exercise meaningful control over the conduct of their lives. Numerous explanations might be given for this. The rise of supranational institutions have tended to remove political power from nations and their citizens. Governments and their citizens often seem subject to worldwide economic trends over which they are able to exercise little or no control. Within individual nations developments such as corporate structures tended to limit the power exercised by individual members of the public.

One further explanation which might be offered for this sense of powerlessness concerns inadequate mechanisms of accountability to ensure that those who make decisions on issues of public policy are adequately answerable for the decisions which they take and the services they deliver. Below we select Britain as a case study to discuss a number of key developments affecting the accountability of those concerned with public policy.

The role of national government

The role of national government expanded in post-war Britain, sometimes to the detriment of the provision of services by local government. In particular, the development of the welfare state resulted in a wider range of functions being performed on behalf of citizens who were not greatly involved in the planning or administration of them. Indeed, it has often been argued that the welfare services were primarily shaped by the concerns of those who carried them out rather than by the needs of those who were meant to benefit from them. This became an increasingly acute problem as factors such as increased education made it feasible for increased widespread popular involvement in public affairs.

Privatisation

Numerous contemporary developments concerning the implementation of public services have compounded the problems referred to above. Policies such as privatisation have taken services such as gas, water and electricity out of the public sector and led to them being discharged by private companies. Although subject to some degree of supervision by regulatory agencies, such bodies were not politically accountable to those who utilised such services but became answerable to their shareholders. Their former political accountability to the public was replaced by consumerism – citizens became customers who theoretically had the ability to go elsewhere if a company did not act as they desired.

Quangos

British governments have also increasingly transferred functions from public bodies such as local government to quangos which are not politically accountable to the public (save in a very indirect sense by virtue of being accountable to those politicians who appointed them). Here accountability tends to be of the managerial variety, secured by processes such as auditing. But there is no public involvement in determining the policies or priorities of such bodies.

Loss of confidence in political parties

Why factors might explain reduced public confidence in the operations of political parties?

A further problem affecting people's confidence in conventional political activity is concerned with the operations of political parties.

Numerous fears have been expressed within liberal democracies that the established institutions of government have failed to meet public expectations. Here we concentrate on the performance of political parties. Many countries have seen evidence of distrust and alienation being demonstrated by the public towards those organisations which play a key role in the conduct of political affairs. This may be explained by a number of factors which are discussed below.

Inefficiency

Fears have been expressed that parties are unable to 'deliver the goods': that is they make extravagant promises during election campaigns which they are unable to fulfil if returned to office. During the 1970s the 'overload' thesis was put forward as an explanation of this problem in Britain. It was argued that in order to win elections political parties were forced to outbid their opponents and make promises which they could not keep due to the diminishing resources of the state to finance such ever-increasing demands. The result was popular disillusionment with the performance of political parties based on the perception that they were either inefficient or dishonest. These sentiments were sometimes reinforced by a belief that parties lacked the capacity to effectively address contemporary political problems.

Avoidance of key issues

There was also a belief that political parties sometimes avoided what many citizens believed to be key issues of concern. Issues such as the protection of the environment did not always figure as prominently in party manifestos as many people wished. This led to a rise in support for single-issue politics which were frequently conducted by pressure groups rather than mainstream political parties.

Consensus

Parties were further accused of moving closer together in terms of both ideology and policies. Left-wing parties in particular seemed to undergo significant reforms. During the 1980s the British Labour Party embarked upon a number of changes affecting its ideology, policy and organisation which indicated an abandonment of fundamentalist socialism while the New Zealand Labour Party adopted Thatcherite monetarist economic policies after 1984. This approach was styled 'Rogernomics' after the Minister of Finance, Roger Douglas. However, the perception that parties of the Left and Right were drawing closer together raised the question as to whether parties really 'mattered'.

Disunity

Party disunity might also be cited as an explanation for the loss of confidence in political parties. They sometimes seem preoccupied with their own internal disputes which may affect the actions of the leadership and the contents of party policy.

THE 1995 CONSERVATIVE LEADERSHIP CONTEST

In 1995 the British prime minister, John Major, highlighted divisions within his own party by inviting his opponents to 'put up or shut up'. This triggered a leadership contest in which 89 Conservative Members of Parliament declined to support him and voted for his opponent, John Redwood. Subsequent statements by the prime minister, especially in connection with the issue of a single European currency following the 1995 Madrid summit meeting, seemed designed to placate Eurosceptic fears concerning economic and monetary union.

'Hypocrisy'

Political parties are sometimes accused of advocating courses of action to the general public to which their own leading members do not subscribe. In Britain prime minister John Major's 1993 'Back to Basics' campaign, in which traditional Conservative values of self-discipline and the importance of the family were emphasised, was undermined by accusations that such values were not personally adhered to by all members of the Conservative parliamentary party. Similarly, the decision by a leading member of Labour's Shadow Cabinet to send her son to a selective grammar school in early 1996 was criticised on the grounds that it seemed out of line with the policy advocated by the party on this issue.

Loss of confidence in public officials

What implications do allegations of inappropriate behaviour by public officials have for a liberal democratic political system?

A final issue for us to consider in connection with the vitality of liberal democracy is concerned with the conduct of those who are elected to public office. We have argued that the system of representative democracy involves citizens electing public officials to serve in the legislative and executive branches of government. Their role is to put forward the views of those who elected them to office. However, it is sometimes alleged that the main concern of elected public office holders is to use their positions to further their own interests or those of people who are close to them. Accusations of conflict of interest, abuse of power or corruption have been levelled against elected officials in many countries. In 1995 many liberal democracies were rocked by such allegations.

The Italian elder statesman and seven-times prime minister, Giulio Andreotti, was placed on trial for 'mafia conspiracy' (that is, using his political power to shield members of this organisation). A former prime minister, Silvio Berlusconi, was tried for corruption on the allegation that he bribed tax inspectors who audited his publishing and television companies' books. One of his senior aides, Francesco Musotto, was charged with mafia conspiracy. A former foreign minister, Gianni de Michelis, was jailed for four years for corruption.

The French prime minister, Alain Juppé, was accused of abusing his position as deputy mayor of Paris to secure low-cost accommodation for himself and his family, although no prosecution arose in this case. However, the Belgian Parliament's decision to lift the immunity of a former defence minister, Guy Coeme, and a former minister for economic affairs, Willy Claes, in a case involving corruption, led to the latter's resignation as Secretary-General of NATO. This accusation alleged the payment of bribes to the Flemish socialist party by companies seeking government defence contracts. The Belgium foreign minister, Frank Vandenbroucke, also resigned over this issue in 1995.

In America the Iran–Contra affair had an adverse effect on the credibility of the Reagan presidency in its later years and resulted in the new incumbent, President Clinton, promising to provide an 'ethical administration'. However this aim was adversely affected by a number of scandals involving leading members of his cabinet and by the involvement of President Clinton and his wife in a real estate venture in Arkansas ('Whitewater') which became the subject of a Congressional probe in 1995. This problem escalated in early 1996 when the president's wife was subpoenaed to appear before a federal grand jury, and a federal judge subpoenaed the president to personally appear as a witness in a criminal trial connected with this episode.

In Spain the Supreme Court launched an investigation into accusations that the prime minister, Felipe González, was involved in the death squads which operated against Basque separatists in the mid-1980s. One of his close associates, José Barrionuevo (who was Interior Minister at the time), was stripped of his parliamentary immunity to enable him to be tried for involvement in such activities.

Allegations against public officials are not always substantiated. Indeed, they may be maliciously made for political reasons. But it is important that those elected to public office should act honestly and that mechanisms should exist within liberal democratic structures of government to investigate (and if necessary punish) those whose integrity is found to be lacking. For if the general public feel that the main aim of seeking election to public office is to pursue self-interest rather than advance the needs of constituents or the interests of the nation, the prestige of elected officials suffers. Ultimately the legitimacy of the system of liberal democracy may be undermined. In this section we investigate the measures taken by legislatures in Britain and Canada to uphold high standards in public life.

Sleaze – the British experience

During the 1990s accusations of improper conduct have been levelled against members of the executive and legislative branches of government. The issue of arms sales to Iran and Iraq by British companies posed major problems for members of the government. The collapse of a trial against one such company, Matrix Churchill, in 1992 resulted in the appointment of an inquiry headed by Lord Justice Scott. A key concern was whether ministers privately agreed to the relaxation of restrictions on the sale of arms to Iraq while leading Parliament and the public to believe that no change of policy had been initiated. This alleged duplicity was associated with the use of Public Immunity Certificates to cover up such a situation in trials of companies accused of engaging in such a trade. The government survived a parliamentary vote on the Scott report in February 1996 by a margin of one.

A further issue arose in 1994 when two Conservative Members of Parliament were accused of accepting money to table parliamentary questions to ministers in the House of Commons. It was subsequently alleged that two additional Members had been paid by a lobbyist to ask parliamentary questions. These episodes suggested that some Members of Parliament had used their positions for personal gain. The prime minister responded by appointing a 'Committee on Standards in Public Life', chaired by Lord Nolan. It issued its report in 1995.

The Nolan Committee's report was broadly supportive of the standards which existed in British public life but it indicated that there was some public concern over the conduct of people involved in public affairs and that this had increased in recent years. The report thus urged action to ensure that corruption and malpractice did not become an accepted aspect of public affairs in Britain. To achieve this goal, the Committee put forward seven principles of public life. These were selflessness, integrity, objectivity, accountability, openness, honesty and leadership. The report then made a number of specific recommendations to govern the subsequent behaviour of elected officials.

It was proposed that Members of Parliament should be prohibited from acting as consultants to lobbying companies. Consultancies to other bodies, such as commercial organisations, would be permitted but become subject to enhanced scrutiny. The Committee recommended that Members would be required to make a full entry in the Register of Members' Interests of all contracts which they secured as a result of being a Member of Parliament and the amount they were paid for the services they provided. The report also suggested that parliament's self-regulation (by the Select Committee on Members' Interests and the Privileges Committee) should cease and that an independent Parliamentary Commissioner should be appointed. This official would maintain the Register of Members' Interests, give advice to Members on matters of conduct and would investigate allegations of misconduct. The House of Commons' Privileges Committee would, however, continue to be responsible for the punishment meted out to any Member found guilty of misbehaviour.

The Nolan Committee was not solely concerned with the behaviour of members of the legislative branch of government. Curbs on the appointment powers of ministers to quangos were proposed and it was recommended that a Public Appointments Commissioner should monitor bias in the membership of such bodies, thus providing a safeguard against 'jobs for the boys'. It argued that former cabinet ministers should be subject to the same vetting rules as senior civil servants before they could take up jobs in the private sector in areas in which they had a direct ministerial involvement. This would involve a mandatory waiting period of three months and independent vetting of any job offered within two years of leaving office. The aim of such restrictions was to ensure that ex-ministers could not be accused of using former contacts to further the interests of the organisation which they joined when they ceased to hold public office.

The prime minister referred the implementation of the report to a special Select Committee of the House of Commons. Many of the Nolan Committee's recommendations were endorsed but the majority of the Committee was unwilling to sanction approval of disclosure of income derived from consultancy work. However, the report and the Select Committee's responses were subsequently put to the full House of Commons. In November 1995 the House decided to support the Nolan report and voted that Members would have to declare all income which arose from their position as Members of Parliament.

RULES GOVERNING MPs' BEHAVIOUR

Following the publication of the Nolan report in 1995 the House of Commons voted to introduce new rules governing the behaviour of MPs. These were the response to allegations of 'sleaze' which had been made previously. The main innovations were:

1 MPs were required to disclose earnings from all consultancies which arose from their position as an MP.
2 MPs were to be prohibited from tabling amendments, motions or questions on behalf of outside interests: the practice known as 'paid advocacy'.
3 A Parliamentary Commissioner for Standards (Sir George Downey) would be appointed. MPs would register all details of contracts with this official.
4 A code of practice was approved in principle.

The House of Lords also voted to set up a register of peers' financial interests.

The Canadian response to 'conflict of interest'

'Conflict of interest' arises when a legislator's private interest impinge on his or her public duties. In Canada a report by Justice William Parker of the Ontario Supreme Court asserted that a former cabinet minister, the Hon. Sinclair Stevens, had breached the Canadian Conflict of Interest Rules on 14 occasions between September 1985 and May 1986. This prompted the establishment of a Special Joint Committee of the House of Commons and the Senate which tabled recommendations in 1992.

This committee proposed the consolidation of existing conflict of interest rules into one piece of legislation. It recommended that an independent official – the Jurisconsult – should be appointed to oversee the disclosure of assets and liabilities by members of both Houses, investigate alleged breaches of the Act relating to disclosure, and advise parliamentarians in this area. The report also urged that clear procedures should be introduced to require members not to vote on issues in which they had an interest. A further suggestion was that members should, to the best of their ability, declare the assets of their spouses.

The future for liberal democracy

Why do the issues raised above pose fundamental threats to liberal democracy?

The above factors suggest that large numbers of people are unhappy with the operations of liberal democratic political systems. Large areas of activity affecting the public are not subject to political accountability, political parties may operate in such a manner that they do not serve popular needs and politicians are sometimes accused of putting self-interest before public service.

Such perceptions, if widely held, threaten to undermine public support for the institutions and processes of the liberal democratic state. In many countries citizens are increasingly willing to use self-help and/or direct action to secure objectives which are important to them even if this means confronting government or its agencies such as the police. For them, conventional political activity is seen as an ineffective mechanism for furthering their interests. This perception may undermine people's trust in government and develop into a belief that this is an expensive interference into people's everyday lives.

Direct action and self-help can be viewed as an important aspect of the liberal democratic political process. However, if increasing reliance becomes placed on this means of activity other conventional methods of political conduct become downgraded. This may result in the authority of the government being questioned and its power challenged by those willing to meet the threat of sanction with force. An extreme example of this rejection of government is found in American militia movements which seek to reassert the rights of the people over what are seen as the unwarranted intrusions of government.

Questions

1 With reference to any country with which you are familiar, assess the argument that in recent years citizens have lost control over the conduct of their everyday lives.
2 Why have the operations of political parties been subject to criticism in many liberal democracies? How valid do you consider these criticisms to be?
3 Devise a code to ensure that elected public officials subscribe to standards of behaviour in public life which you feel to be desirable.
4 'Citizens have lost confidence in politicians and government.' To what extent do you agree with this statement and what dangers does it pose for liberal democracy?

Summary

1 In recent years numerous criticisms have been levelled at the conduct of politics in liberal democracies.
2 World economic trends and the rise of supranational institutions have resulted in governments and their citizens experiencing a loss of power in the conduct of their everyday affairs. Citizens, however, may have been adversely affected by political developments within their own country.
3 In Britain, for example, the power exerted by professionals who deliver services to the public and the increasing tendency to administer public services by private companies and quangos which are inadequately politically accountable for their actions has aggravated feelings of powerlessness by the general public.
4 In a number of liberal democracies there has been a loss of

confidence in political parties. They have been accused of failing to deliver the promises they make during elections and of being preoccupied with internal divisions to the detriment of tackling issues deemed to be important by the public. A tendency for parties in individual countries to pursue similar objectives and policies may be a further explanation for public disenchantment with their operations.

5   In some countries, people's trust in politicians and government has been undermined by allegations of corrupt behaviour by elected officials. In Britain the issue of standards in public life was examined by a committee chaired by Lord Nolan which put forward recommendations to regulate the activities of Members of Parliament.

6   Perceptions of powerlessness, reduced levels of confidence in the operations of political parties and mistrust of politicians has resulted in an increased willingness to utilise direct action to secure political ends by citizens in many liberal democratic states. This development may reduce support for conventional political activity and, in an extreme form, may undermine people's trust and respect for government.

FURTHER READING

Having secured some basic information concerning the operations of liberal democratic political systems in the First world, you are in a position to expand your knowledge. The following books will help you to do this.

Rod Hague, Martin Harrop and Shaun Breslin, *Comparative Government and Politics*, (Basingstoke: Macmillan, 1992, 3rd edition).

> This is a clearly written, authoritative text. The information which it contains on Second and Third World countries will particularly broaden your understanding and knowledge of politics.

Andrew Heywood, *Political Ideas and Concepts*, (Basingstoke: Macmillan, 1994).

> This is an excellent book covering a wide range of issues which are involved in the study of political theory. Its particular merit is its ability to discuss quite complex matters in a lucid manner which is readily understandable to those with little grounding in this subject area.

M. Donald Hancock, David Conradt, B. Guy Peters, William Safran and Raphael Zariski, *Politics in Western Europe*, (Chatham, New Jersey: Chatham House Publishers, 1993).

> This book provides a useful comparative account of politics in Britain, France, Germany, Italy and Sweden in which power is utilised as the focus of analysis. It also contains a chapter on the European Union.

Clive S. Thomas (editor), *First World Interest Groups, A Comparative Perspective*, (Westport, Connecticut: Greenwood Press, 1993).

This work provides a thorough investigation of the role performed by pressure groups in public policy making in 12 Western liberal democracies. It seeks to assess the similarities and differences in group activity in countries which include America, Canada, New Zealand, Australia and Britain.

Additionally, the following national studies will enhance your knowledge of political affairs in individual countries:

Robert Pyper and Lynton Robins, *Governing the UK in the 1990s*, (Basingstoke: Macmillan, 1995)

David McKay, *American Politics and Society*, (Oxford: Blackwell, 1993, 3rd edition)

Edwin Coulter, *Principles of Politics and Government*, (Dubuque, Iowa: William Brown, 1991, 4th edition). Although this work thoroughly addresses many of the underlying themes and concepts related to the study of politics, much of the subject matter is drawn from America.

Peter Morris, *French Politics Today*, (Manchester: Manchester University Press, 1994).

Basil Chubb, *The Government and Politics of Ireland*, (London: Longman, 1992, 3rd edition).

Ralph Negrine, *Politics and the Mass Media in Britain*, (London: Routledge, 1994, 2nd edition).

INDEX